THE SKINNERS' SCHOOL

Its controversial birth
and
its landmark buildings

Cecil Beeby
and
Philip Whitbourn

Royal Tunbridge Wells Civic Society
Local History Monograph No. 3

Published by
The Royal Tunbridge Wells Civic Society
2004

Published in Great Britain in October 2004 by
The Local History Group of
The Royal Tunbridge Wells Civic Society

ISBN No. 0 – 9545343 – 2 - 8

The text is set in Bookman Old Style 10 pt.
and the front cover in Bookman Old Style 16 pt.

Front cover: The West Tower, The Skinners' School
Back cover: Gate pier, showing the arms of the
Worshipful Company of Skinners

Printed and bound by the Ink Pot Lithographic Printers,
Southborough, Tunbridge Wells, Kent TN4 OLT

CONTENTS

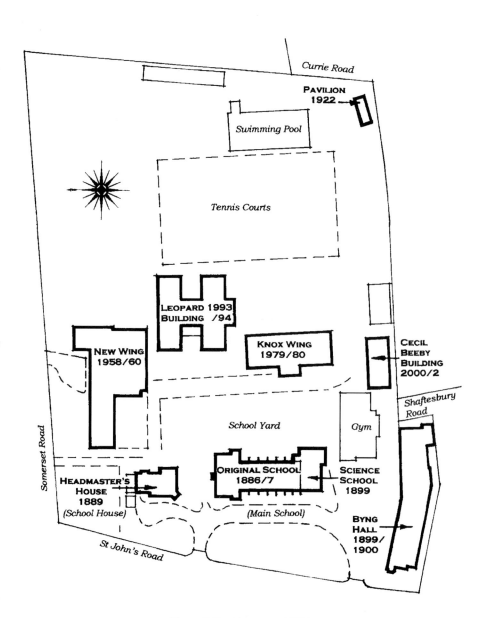

Plan of the Campus, 2004

INTRODUCTION

Almost exactly twenty years ago, back in September 1984, the late Cecil Beeby, a much-respected former Headmaster of The Skinners' School, Tunbridge Wells, published an account of the bringing into being of the school under the title "The Birth of a School, or A Tale of Two Townships". In this he described Victorian rivalries between Tunbridge Wells and its near-neighbour Tonbridge town, which he saw as a "period piece", and as a "cameo" of the pride and persistence of the age.

Sadly, it is a "cameo" that has become out of print, and thus one that is no longer readily available to those who may be interested in this "period piece". The Society is therefore grateful to his widow, Muriel Beeby, for kindly agreeing to the reprinting of the account as part of its Monograph series, covering different aspects of the history of Royal Tunbridge Wells. Cecil Beeby's text has been reproduced without alteration, and the chapter entitled "Today" remains as true as it was two decades ago.

To the story of the birth of the School, I have added a note on its older buildings and architectural features, which it is hoped may prove of interest too.

The Society is grateful also to the present Headmaster, Peter Braggins; the Bursar, John Hann; and to the Worshipful Company of Skinners for their encouragement in the enterprise as well, of course, as to the several Society members who have contributed to the undertaking in various ways.

In particular, Mary Woodruffe has kindly typed my contribution and, as ever, the Local History Group's Hon. Secretary, John Cunningham, has played a leading part in the production process.

Philip Whitbourn, OBE,
President, Royal Tunbridge Wells Civic Society
Chairman, Local History Group, Royal Tunbridge Wells Civic Society

September 2004

PART I

THE BIRTH OF A SCHOOL
or
A TALE OF TWO TOWNSHIPS

CHAPTER 1
THE FORCES MUSTER

It can scarcely be said that The Skinners' School had an easy birth. To those eagerly awaiting its arrival, it must have seemed an unconscionable time appearing. Nor did its parents seem to have greeted its birth with conspicuous delight, or even modified rapture.

The trouble was that, as many of its family believed, it was being built in the wrong place — and under duress. It is hard to avoid the conclusion that, in certain quarters, it received such a limited welcome as would commonly have been given to the illegitimate offspring of a proud and noble house. In its formative years it would certainly be expected to observe its proper station.

For, as many other contemporary day schools, it was openly planned to be a Middle or Second Grade foundation, its curriculum more suited to the sons of the tradesmen, as its potential pupils were regularly described, and correspondingly limited in its scope and aspirations.

In brief, The Skinners School was a product of the Endowed Schools Reform movement of the mid-19th century. It sprang essentially from the response of the Worshipful Company of Skinners, sole Governors of Tonbridge School since the death in 1558 of that school's founder, Sir Andrew Judd, to the pressures applied by the Schools Enquiry Commissioners by Act of Parliament appointed.

Reform indeed had long been in the air. Mismanagement, neglect and commonly corruption could readily be instanced in the affairs of many long established schools. The Free Grammar School of Sir Andrew Judd, more commonly known today as Tonbridge School, however well governed, could in no way escape the Commissioners' scrutiny. Nor were the Commissioners alone in pressing for reform of that school's arrangements. Both Headmaster and assistant masters, many parents and other interested parties appreciated the need to modernize its curriculum, to provide for the teaching of science and generally to broaden the base of boys' studies. Many, too, pressed for the abolition of the exclusive claims of local boys to the generous university awards at the governors' disposal. Not that encroachment upon such privilege, or any action to encourage or expand the school's boarding element, could conceivably be achieved without vigorous reaction on the part of the local population.

Lord Mayor of London in 1550, Master of his City Livery Company no fewer than six times, having founded his school in his native town, Sir Andrew Judd had willed its governance in future years to the Master, Wardens and Brethren of that same Company, of which he had been so distinguished a member. His intentions, as the Commissioners' report of 1867 noted, had been twofold: to provide free instruction in grammar to boys residing in Tonbridge and the adjacent country *(in dicta villa et patria ibidem adjacente);* and to benefit the town by bringing boarders to the houses of the Headmaster and of the inhabitants.

With no single day boy in attendance at the time of the Commissioners' enquiry from beyond the borders of Tonbridge town itself, the Commissioners were inevitably concerned regarding the school's service to the adjacent country. Equally inevitably the question arose as to how a school expanding its boarding provision at the expense of the locality, could redress the balance and more fully satisfy local needs.

In the meantime the sharp increase anticipated in the school's income in the years immediately ahead was noted. Its revenue was estimated by Mr. Gladstone, when Chancellor of the Exchequer, as likely to rise to £80,000 per annum early in the next century, and at £20,000 by the more cautious school authorities. It would probably, as the Commissioners tartly observed, "much exceed the latter estimate." Furthermore, the report insisted, the composition of the school's governing body should be revised to include an equal representation of local interests alongside the Skinners' Company's members.

Plainly the Skinners' Company now had much to consider. It had also the right to reply and to submit a scheme of its own to the Commissioners for the future running of its school. It is in the Company's proposals of 1870, or more correctly in a memorandum attached to these proposals, that the germ first appears of what in the fullness of much time became The Skinners' School.

It is quite impossible to trace the beginnings of The Skinners' School in Tunbridge Wells without much reference to Tonbridge School. It must, however, be observed at once that any reference in these pages to the succession of schemes and counter schemes for the administration of Tonbridge School, will seek to concentrate on those elements only of such schemes as are relevant to our present purpose. Much else concerning Tonbridge School's curriculum, staffing, scholarship awards and other matters has little direct bearing upon our present subject.

Thus of the many elements in the Tonbridge School Governors' own primary concern; the proposal by the governors to found a Second Grade School "at Tonbridge or in some adjacent locality", provided they were enabled to endow this out of certain funds arising from the residuary estate of Sir Thomas Smythe, a major charitable trust still administered by the Skinners' Company, and from other funds held by the Company. To balance this generous intention the opening clause of the governors' proposals asserted very firmly indeed that the Skinners' Company and its successors should continue sole governors of Tonbridge School.

Tonbridge School in the early 1860s

The scene indeed was set, the battle lines drawn for the tussle between Company and Commissioners, and very soon between Tonbridge and Tunbridge Wells, which finally after exceeding travail, saw The Skinners' School's birth seventeen years later.

Pressure for "Middle Schools" — for the benefit of the sons of the middle classes — was widespread and mounting. With the better provision for the lower classes envisaged by the Education Act of 1870, articulate sections of the tradesman community increasingly expressed themselves frustrated and neglected. The Tunbridge Wells Gazette in October 1870 crisply summed up this feeling. "Upper and Lower classes have been cared for in the matter of education, the former by the endowed schools, the latter by the state national schools; the middle classes have been left to get an education as best they could."

By proposing a Second Grade School alongside Tonbridge School, the governors of the existing school were certainly in tune with the times, and for the moment their local critics generally were silenced.

Hopes were moreover raised two years later, in November 1872, when Mr. Latham, an Assistant Commissioner for Endowed Schools, visited Tonbridge to canvass local opinion regarding a new school's foundation and other matters implicit in the Governors scheme for their existing school. Subsequently a public meeting in Tonbridge, chaired by Mr. Homersham Cox, barrister and prominent Old Tonbridgian resident, approved the despatch of a letter to the Commissioners urging acceptance of the governors' offer and their retention as sole governors of their school.

Tonbridge residents, however, were not the only participants in this public meeting. Stirrings were now evident beyond Tonbridge town's borders, and in neighbouring Tunbridge Wells especially, there were those who demanded that that town too should share in any expansion of the area's educational provision.

Why should the new school not be sited in Tunbridge Wells?
Was not Tunbridge Wells by far the larger town?
Was not Tunbridge Wells "in the adjacent country" in the terms of Sir Andrew Judd's original foundation?

Tunbridge Wells Old Town Hall

An earlier meeting had accordingly been convened in Tunbridge Wells Town Hall on the eve of the Tonbridge gathering, with the aim of securing for the larger town a share in any benefit deriving from change in Tonbridge School's administration. With the Honourable F.G. Molyneux presiding and the redoubtable Canon Hoare, Vicar of Holy Trinity Church, prominent in the discussions, these two gentlemen together with the Rev. George Jones, Minister of Emmanuel Church, and Mr. Gibson were appointed delegates to attend the Tonbridge meeting.

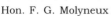

Hon. F. G. Molyneux   Canon Hoare   Revd. George Jones

At this stage Tunbridge Wells' opinion, as expressed in the earlier meeting, was by no means unanimous in pressing for a second school. Many would have been content with an adjustment by Tonbridge School of the very early hour at which it began its day.

A later start permitting attendance by Tunbridge Wells boys would have satisfied them. Alternatively a "branch" school for younger pupils leading to Tonbridge School in later years might well, it was suggested, meet Tunbridge Wells needs.

The presence of a Tunbridge Wells deputation at the Tonbridge meeting was, however, patently unwelcome to the older town. In its representation to the Endowed Schools Commissioners despatched in May 1873 the Tonbridge Committee, appointed at that town's meeting, sought to deal firmly with Tunbridge Wells' proposals for any new establishment in Tunbridge Wells. "It is clear from the original instruments that Sir Andrew Judd, though he intended to provide for the education of children in the country adjacent to Tonbridge, did not contemplate the establishment of a school in any other place. There is not one word in these documents to justify the diversion of funds which the deputation from Tunbridge Wells sought."

At the same time, the Tonbridge spokesmen were at pains to stress that they had no serious complaint regarding the Skinners' Company's exercise of its right to govern Tonbridge School. If the Commissioners insisted on change in the Governing Body's composition, any outside appointments, they suggested, should be as assessors or advisers only, not as voting governors. With Tonbridge School funds, however, mounting apace, the establishment of a Second Grade School, whether in the town itself or in the immediate vicinity, would solve most of the difficulties regarding the application of these funds and be of the utmost value to the large majority of tradesmen, as it was submitted, "who do not require a higher mathematical or classical education for their children."

It is of interest that elsewhere in their representation the Tonbridge spokesmen stoutly rejected any thought that the funds for a new school should be found by increasing Tonbridge School fees. In an intriguing glimpse of contemporary attitudes it is crisply commented that "the principle of taxing one class of the community for the benefit of another class is utterly indefensible."

One slight alteration in the present school's routine would, however, be welcomed. As Tunbridge Wells spokesmen had earlier pressed, could not the school begin its working day later? Chapel at 7 am. in summer and 7.30 a.m. in winter effectively confined day boy attendance to those living within about one mile. In certain public schools, it was observed similar early starts to their day had been established with the avowed intention of excluding day boys and becoming exclusively boarding institutions. In any new scheme for Tonbridge School all such arrangements should be expressly prohibited. In conclusion, the Tonbridge spokesmen — Messrs. Homersham Cox, William Gorham, Joseph Isard and the delightfully named Gentle Brown — again stressed the "unanimous sentiment" of the people of Tonbridge as to the high standing of Tonbridge School, its excellent discipline and the calibre of its masters.

For about two years at this point, little transpired. By a regular series of articles on Tonbridge School, both past and present, the radical editor of the Tonbridge Free Press, Mr. William Blair, sought indeed to sustain his readers' interest in the school's arrangements and to nurture their hopes of a new foundation more in accord with the locality's needs. By early 1874, however, even the indefatigable Mr. Blair felt compelled to suspend his observations, promising nonetheless to resume them "when an altered prospect gives a new interest in the project."

In the meantime, the Commissioners had indicated to the Skinners' Company that its intention to draw on the Smythe Charity to fund any new foundation, would not be permissible under existing law. Furthermore the Endowed Schools Commission itself, having run its allotted span, was in process of handing over its business to the Charity Commissioners with some inevitable loss of time and momentum.

Not that the Tonbridge committee had been wholly inactive. In May 1874 it had addressed another long and closely reasoned appeal to the Endowed Schools Commissioners, summarizing local feeling and stressing its belief that a Second Grade School would satisfy most of its fellow townsmen. A question furthermore had been asked in the House of Commons in the following month by Mr. Julian Goldsmid, MP for Rochester, as to the delay in proposing a new scheme for Tonbridge School — an enquiry doubtless prompted by the Tonbridge committee. More than four years had indeed elapsed since that new school had appeared just over the horizon. It was time for another Public Meeting in Tonbridge Town Hall. Delayed for a month by its chairman's bronchitis, it was eventually assembled on the first day of February 1875.

Once again, Mr. Homersham Cox succinctly summarized the main issues involved. Whilst the Skinners' Company's governance of its school was generally satisfactory, there was nonetheless a need for some local representation upon the Governing Body. Morning school should certainly start later. The prime requirement, however, remained the establishment of a Second Grade or Commercial School. Not a single tradesman's son was currently attending Tonbridge School.

As ever, discussion ranged over a wide and varied field. Much was again said of the need to modernize Tonbridge School's curriculum, boarding arrangements, fees and much else. General agreement, however, prevailed as to the urgent need for a new school. But founded where?

Increasingly the interpretation of Sir Andrew Judd's wishes became the focus of attention. The small Tunbridge Wells contingent in attendance would certainly not yield its claims to a share in the founder's benefaction. The Rev. George Jones maintained vigorously that 'Tonbridge' meant the whole parish of Tonbridge, an area embracing the greater part of Tunbridge Wells, albeit some five miles distant.

Those who spoke for Tunbridge Wells indeed were more than ready for a fight, indignant as they were, that no notice of the meeting had been circulated in Tunbridge Wells. Nor could they be happy with the composition of the new committee appointed, or re-appointed, to convey the feeling of the meeting to the Charity Commissioners and the Skinners' Company, whenever occasion offered or required.

The distinguished names of the Honourable F.G. Molyneux and Sir David Salomons as would-be Tunbridge Wells representatives were, however, roughly cast aside. When, furthermore, an amendment to the meeting's principal motion demanded Tonbridge Town as the hoped for new school's site, amid much ill natured wrangling and most uncertain voting, the meeting concluded in manifest disorder.

Even the Tonbridge Free Press, predisposed as its editor was to support his fellow townsmen, whether the foemen be the Commissioners, the Skinners' Company or the intruding gentlemen from Tunbridge Wells, reported the uproar at the meeting's end in the most scathing terms.

At an earlier point in the proceedings, the names of Messrs. Charles Pugh and Frank East are recorded in the lengthy report of the meeting as being nominated to lend their additional weight to the town's committee. In his concluding word, however, Mr. Blair can but characterise the proceedings as "the merest farce", adding that "no one was so clearly appointed as to warrant us giving names."

TUNBRIDGE WELLS
AND THE
TUNBRIDGE
GRAMMAR SCHOOL.

A PUBLIC
MEETING

Of the Inhabitants of Tunbridge Wells, will be held at the

TOWN HALL,
TUNBRIDGE WELLS,

On THURSDAY next, the 11th instant,
At THREE o'Clock in the Afternoon,

Relative to the Scheme before the Charity Commissioners on the subject of the Endowments of Tunbridge Grammar School, and to consider the desirability of taking steps to secure to Tunbridge Wells and Neighbourhood a share of the Educational advantages to be derived from those Endowments, and to obtain, if possible, the establishment at Tunbridge Wells of a SECOND GRADE SCHOOL in connection therewith.

THE HON. F. G. MOLYNEUX
HAS KINDLY CONSENTED TO PRESIDE.

Feb. 8th, 1878.

By Order of the RATEPAYERS' ASSOCIATION,

FRAS. BOREHAM, *Sec.*

Printed at the "Calverley Printing Works," by HENRY S. COLBRAN, 9, Calverley Road, Tunbridge Wells.

The Call Goes Forth.

Meanwhile the gentlemen from Tunbridge Wells had stumped off home, not so much to lick their wounds as to prepare their own town's case and to prime their own guns. Within days the citizens of Tunbridge Wells found themselves summoned to their own meeting in their own Town Hall. Bidden as they were by the town's Ratepayers' Association, at the instance of Mr. Francis Boreham, its secretary, the gentlemen of Tunbridge Wells were duly invited in their turn "to consider the desirability of taking steps to secure to Tunbridge Wells a participation in the educational advantages of Tonbridge School and to obtain, if possible, the establishment in Tunbridge Wells of a Second Grade School in connection therewith".

With the Honourable F. G. Molyneux presiding, the superior claims of Tunbridge Wells not surprisingly were vigorously presented and whole-heartedly endorsed. Mr Wilson of Southborough indeed pressed that the matter should be pursued in a friendly spirit with no overt break with their Tonbridge neighbours. Might not funds be made available for two schools, one in each town? Mr. Wilson's mediation, however, won little support. Meanwhile population statistics bounced to and fro. Was not Tunbridge Wells more than twice the size of Tonbridge? Was it not moreover almost wholly within the parish of Tonbridge?

If the Rev. George Jones' figures were to be believed, it certainly was the larger town. Claiming a total population for Tunbridge Wells town itself within "a radius of two miles from Trinity Church" of 18,300, and adding thereto 2767 for Rusthall, 3583 for Southborough and 314 for the part of Frant in Kent, he mustered a final figure of 24,964 souls. Against this Tonbridge could boast, he asserted, no more than 9641, with 8209 only in Tonbridge itself, bolstered by 1182 in Hildenborough and a modest 250 in Bidborough as well. Did not everyone know furthermore that Tunbridge Wells' situation was far more salubrious than fog and flood-riven Tonbridge? The good citizens of Tunbridge Wells were in no doubt at all that, if any new school was to be founded, it should be in Tunbridge Wells. So too, whatever might be the views of the Tonbridge Free Press or any other organ, Tunbridge Wells' own Gazette lent its full support to its own town's claims, and happily printed correspondence echoing the enthusiasm, even the euphoria of the hour. Could not the names of potential pupils be canvassed at once, demanded the anonymous YZ, if a school could be opened, say at Easter 1876?

The powerful committee appointed to represent Tunbridge Wells' interests, comprising the Honourable F. G. Molyneux, the Rev. Canon Hoare, the Rev. George Jones, Messrs. F. Argyle and W. F. Browell and others involved in the commercial and professional life of the town, was launched indeed on its task with the highest hopes. The last two named gentlemen could scarcely have envisaged that they would be equally involved in battle in some ten and more years' time. It would be all over in a matter of months. As another of the Gazette's correspondents saw it, "with a good working committee and perhaps the addition of a few good names to the present list, Tunbridge Wells, one would think, cannot fail to succeed."

Mr. F. Argyle

There were, no doubt, some in Tunbridge Wells who could foresee the bitter warfare which would ensue with their Tonbridge neighbours.

Mr. W. F. Browell

Within weeks the Gazette's leader writer, whilst vigorously maintaining his town's claims, regretted nonetheless the bone of contention now arising, and would have been glad to have seen joint action prevailing. Things by now, however, had gone too far, and within a fortnight the Tunbridge Wells Tradesmen's Association at its regular monthly meeting fanned the flames further by resolving to send its own memorial to the Charity Commissioners, having learned "with surprise" of Tonbridge's claim to expropriate, as it expressed it, the whole of the available endowment by a second school in Tonbridge. "A visit to the locality from anyone of your honourable body", the Association urged, "would show that, excepting here and there, there is scarcely any population around Tonbridge".

Not that Tonbridge would yield its claims without battle. Even as the Tradesmen lent their shoulders to the wheel, the men of Tonbridge found themselves summoned yet again to a Town Hall meeting, not least, as it appeared, to ratify the appointment of those somewhat uncertainly nominated as the town's own committee at the earlier meeting. Mr. Blair's press comment is terse indeed; if the committee were earlier appointed, why need confirmation? There should certainly be no need for long speeches at this further meeting. The town would expect the gentlemen wishing to be confirmed to show they had some practical ideas.

The composition of the town's committee was duly established, the name of Colonel Edward Hall being associated with those previously mentioned. Again moreover, debate encompassed other Tonbridge School issues beyond the establishment and siting of another school. Nor was it in all respects as harmonious a gathering as its callers had envisaged. Dispute broke out at the outset, when opposition arose to Mr Homersham Cox's occupation of the chair. There were those present to whom the composition of Tonbridge School's Governing Body was a much more urgent matter than any other issue. Champion as he was of the Skinners' Company's prerogative as the school's sole governors, Mr. Cox was distinctly alarmed and aggrieved. Nor was he re-installed as Chairman before he had threatened to quit the proceedings, unless so approved.

In due time, the newly accredited committee was authorised to press upon the Charity Commissioners an agreed bundle of requests, that for a new school in the town of Tonbridge being partnered by a tempered plea for one or two "assistant governors" to be elected by Tonbridge householders, and the suggestion once again that Tonbridge School's morning hours be modestly amended to permit more day boy attendance.

The year 1875 was plainly to be a harrassing year for the Court of the Skinners' Company, beset as it was by the Charity Commissioners, as they warmed to their work, and irritated no doubt at times by the repeated representations made to it by two rival town communities, competing determinedly for such new school's crumbs as appeared likely to fall from its conceivably richer table.

25th Feb 1875

Tunbridge Grammar School

Sir,

I am instructed to express the Commissioners
regret that they have found it impossible to
answer your letter of the 5th inst. sooner, and
to say that they will be prepared to give their
best consideration to any representations which
may be addressed to them on behalf of the ____
inhabitants of Tunbridge Wells.

Particulars of information respecting the School
will be found in the Report of the Schools
Inquiry Commission (III. 423 and XI. 105) and
in that of the Commissioners of 1819 on the
Education of the Poor (I 149 and Appendix 233)
but the Commissioners are unable to supply
you with copies of these works.

I am, Sir,

Your obedient Servant

D. C. Richmond

Mr. Fras. Borcham
Upper Grosvenor Road
Tunbridge Wells

CHAPTER 2

THE BATTLE OF THE SCHEMES

The month of February 1875 had barely begun, when the Charity Commissioners sought an interview with the Company. The Company's own draft scheme was duly taken down from its shelf and dusted. It was generally agreed within Skinners' Hall that this scheme should in the first instance be the basis of the Company's submission to the Commissioners, subject to minor amendments as, for instance, regarding morning school timing. With a healthy increase too in Tonbridge School's income since 1870, some confidence prevailed that the Company might better afford the cost of a Middle or Second Grade School. There might even be enough for a Girls' School too.

At once, however, the Commissioners made their position very clear. Eager as they were to work in harmony with the Skinners' Company and in no way seriously critical of its management of the school's affairs, with regard to the composition of Tonbridge School's governing body they firmly adhered to their own belief that outsiders should unquestionably form part of its number. *Unquestionably*? Well, perhaps not necessarily so. The Company's own record of its deputation's first encounter with Sir James Hill, the Chief Commissioner for Charities, makes mention of an admission by Sir James that "in certain circumstances the Commissioners might be not unwilling to consider whether Tonbridge School might not be treated as an exceptional case and the Company be permitted to remain the school's sole governors, if the Company were willing out of its own funds, together with funds which could only be made available by the Company's consent, to offer such considerable sums as might justify the Commissioners in so regarding this as an exceptional case."

Specific suggestions indeed were made by the Chief Commissioner as to means whereby the Company from its own funds could relieve the Tonbridge School foundation in order to free part of that school's endowments for a new school. Such new school, he suggested, might well cater for both boys and girls — with a fees pattern favouring those from "Tonbridge District". In a subsequent interview between Sir James and the Master of the Skinners' Company, the

Company were formally invited to submit a proposal of the inducement which it was willing to offer as the price of remaining sole governors.

A bribe? Perhaps. Hints of a possible deal were patently forthcoming, and within Skinners' Hall there were clearly those willing to draw on the Company's own funds — as distinct from the Judd Foundation, the source of Tonbridge School's separate income — to safeguard the Company's unchanged and unassisted governorship of their school.

By mid-April, however, opinion had hardened. A recommendation to seek accommodation with the Commissioners was roundly rejected. The Commissioners should be courteously, but firmly, informed that the Company did not feel disposed to go beyond the proposals submitted to the Endowed Schools Commissioners in 1870. At the same meeting letters were reported from the town committees of both Tonbridge and Tunbridge Wells enclosing copies of communications addressed by each body to the Charity Commissioners, the latter group petitioning for what it described as a" Classical and Commercial School in Tunbridge Wells in connection with and under the care of the governors of the present school."

On receipt of the Company's rejoinder, the Commissioners were understandably affronted. There should be no further delay, they retorted. They would at once take measures to frame a scheme for the regulation of Tonbridge School, bearing in mind the Company's proposals of 1870, but also the wishes and suggestions of persons "locally and otherwise interested", who had addressed them on the subject. Nor was there now any question, as they informed the Company, of the Commissioners yielding an inch with regard to the governing body's constitution. Straining too, as it might appear, to press their views to the limit, the Commissioners were emboldened to suggest that any concession of exclusive governing rights would in fact give the Company more than they had properly possessed in the past. In founding his school, as the Commissioners observed, Sir Andrew Judd had directed that for several important matters "a controlling or concurrent authority" should be exercised by All Souls College, Oxford.   A red herring perhaps. A warning nonetheless that the Commissioners meant business.

Meanwhile a communication from Mr. Homersham Cox with regard to his committee's meeting with the Charity Commissioners in mid-May 1875 may well have encouraged the Company, however much it sowed further seeds of discord between the neighbouring towns. The Commissioners, as Mr. Cox wrote, had indicated their intention within a month to propose a considerable change in the composition of Tonbridge School's governing body. They had none the less enquired of the Tonbridge delegation, whether in the event of the Skinners' Company making a liberal offer for the endowment of a Second Grade School at Tonbridge, the town's inhabitants would forego their claim to share in the government of the present school.

In reply, Mr. Cox and his companions had expressed their own view that at the recent public meeting in Tonbridge the general opinion undoubtedly had been that, whilst such outside governors as the meeting wished to see appointed might usefully confer with the present governors on matters of local interest, it was desirable nonetheless that "the corporate character of the existing Governing Body should continue without any fundamental change". That opinion was based, however, on a belief that the Company was prepared "to demonstrate their great interest in the town by an act of spontaneous munificence". Would the Company, please, assure the town's committee that this intention continued?

If the Company felt unable at this stage to afford any such unequivocal assurance, many among its members must plainly have been encouraged by thoughts of the Tonbridge townsmen's support in any battles ahead. Those townsmen too no doubt returned home quietly confident that a new school would shortly arise within their own town's border.

The Commissioners' draft scheme, however, when it arrived before end of June 1875 satisfied no one. The Governing Body of Tonbridge School was to comprise eight gentlemen only appointed by the Company. Five more would be severally appointed by the Archbishop of Canterbury, by All Souls College, Oxford, by the Lord Lieutenant of Kent, by the magistrates of the County in Quarter Sessions assembled, and by the Archdeacon of Maidstone, together with the Rural Deans of Maidstone Archdeanery. The local representation was to be two resident householders of the parish of Tonbridge rated at not less than £40 per annum.

A Middle School, too, should in due course be established, not from the Smythe funds, but from the steady accumulation over the years of any unapplied surplus income of the present school. Such surplus income was to be deposited with bankers in order that, as suitable sums accrued, they should be invested from time to time in the name of the Official Trustee of Charitable Funds in a separate account termed "The Middle School Fund". In the fullness of time the Company and Tonbridge School's Governing Body should apply to the Charity Commissioners to found and maintain a Middle School "in or near the town of Tonbridge".

Hall of the Skinners' Company,
Dowgate Hill, London

The Company's reaction to theCommissioners' scheme was predictably hostile.

Some were eager to rush through a resolution that, unless the Company were permitted to remain sole governors,it should withdraw from all involvement with its school. Second thoughts, however, prevailed, and succeeding weeks saw the Company engaged in earnest debate and preparation of its reply. Nor could either Tonbridge or Tunbridge Wells possibly be happy with a Middle School dependent upon uncertainly surplus funds and delayed, it could be, for ten, twenty or more years.

This new school'slocation, moreover, "in or near the town of Tonbridge", scarcely reassured Tonbridge townspeople, whatever encouragement it may have given to Tunbridge Wells.

As the Tunbridge Wells news sheet at once observed, the scheme would meet the needs of neither Tunbridge Wells nor Tonbridge: "The question of a Middle School did not appear to have occupied the serious attention of the Commissioners".

In subsequent comment and more grandiloquent terms, the writer deplored the Commissioners' failure to secure the "two fundamental objectives involved — the vindication of the rights of the district to a property held truly to be its own, and the application of sufficient elasticity to the reputedly rapidly rising fortunes of the established school to compensate the district for its virtual exclusion from the present school". The only sop to the locality had been a pair of governors. Bona-fide tradesmen, whom Sir Andrew must have had in mind, as the writer premised, had been completely sacrificed. Tunbridge Wells and Tonbridge should surely unite to gain the Middle School, which seemed now most cruelly to be wrested from their hands.

The Company in the meantime further considered its reply to the Commissioners. Nothing could induce it to yield on the composition of its school's governing body. It sought time, however, for further discussion, and in despatching its own revision of the draft scheme refuting its displacement as sole governors courteously requested another interview with the Commissioners. Before this could be held, Mr. Isard made equally courteous request to the Company for an early interview. With this, the Company were happy to concur without delay. Thus October 14th 1875 saw Messrs. Isard and Gentle Brown again in discussion with the Company together with their colleague, Captain Hall.

Another public meeting had been held in Tonbridge Corn Exchange a month earlier. Encouraged by Mr. Homersham Cox's report of his correspondence and conversation with several of the Company's members, the deputation bore with them specific questions to which they sought the Company's frank answer s. Nor were the Company's spokesmen unprepared with their replies.

An amount of between £10,000 and £15,000, it was answered, had been in the Company's mind, when it first made its proposal in 1870. Such a sum, it was added, was still thought to be sufficient. A scheme of local involvement in, or control of, Tonbridge School's governance by a committee, similar to that lately elected by ratepayers in a like situation elsewhere, would not be acceptable. The Company would, however, have no objection to some local representative body set up to convey to the governors from time to time the views of Tonbridge inhabitants upon matters connected with the two schools envisaged in the 1870 proposals.

Questions and answers concluded, it was intimated to the town's representatives, that the Company remained willing to build and endow a second school at Tonbridge, provided the Charity Commissioners consented to the application to this end of funds referred to in the Company's most recent submission to the Commissioners; and provided also that the Company was satisfied that the inhabitants of the town of Tonbridge opposed the Commissioners' scheme, where it varied in substance from that of the Company.

Returned to Tonbridge, the three emissaries lost no time in summoning another public meeting. A "numerous attendance", as the press reported, assented, if with some dissenting voices, to the Company's proposals. The Commissioners should be pressed forthwith by Tonbridge townsmen to settle on the Company's terms. Whatever grievances the town had nurtured in recent years regarding its divorce from the school in its midst, all could now be forgiven and forgotten as the price of a second school in the town and for the town's own use. If this meant support for the Company's sole government of both schools, so be it.

In London, for several months the Company breathed afresh. Little of import surfaced. Another memorial, signed by some 150 Tonbridge inhabitants, three householders only declining to sign, as the town's newssheet carefully reported, passed from the town to the Commissioners. The prolonged illness, however, of the Chief Commissioner postponed the Commissioners' next meeting with the Company until May 1876. Not that time or sick bed meditation had in any way softened the Commissioners' views. As the Master of the Company reported to his companions, the Commissioners persisted in their view that a body "more varied in its constitution" was likely to work no less efficiently than the existing governors. They furthermore asked from what source, other than the Smythe charity, did the Company propose to find the funds beyond £10,000 for the establishment of a Middle School adequate to the district's needs.

The Company had by this time made plain its intention to draw upon two others of the charitable trust funds within its control, those of Thomas Hunt and Lawrence Atwell, established respectively in 1551 and 1558, to yield the first £10,000 required for a new school's foundation. The Judd Funds too, those earmarked hitherto for the sustenance of the existing school, were growing apace. Leases on properties in Gracechurch Street within the City having fallen in, new leases would yield some additional £1,600 annually in future.

Monument to Sir Andrew Judd
buried at St. Helen's Church,
Bishopsgate on 14th Sept. 1558

From these three sources, the money required could no doubt be raised without undue pain. There were also the Company's own Corporate Funds, and by now the Commissioners were patently hinting that these might need to be called on too.

The Commissioners pressed and gave no hint of quarter. If the Company were to purchase sole governing rights, it must increase its offer by much more yet. The Company for a few months more dug in its toes. If its own unvaried claim were not conceded, it was disposed, as it told the Commission, to take no further steps in founding any other school. Impasse reigned, nor was the Company unduly stirred by further communication from Mr. Homersham Cox enclosing a copy of his fellow townsmen's petition to the House of Commons praying that steps be taken to establish a new scheme without delay, and urging the Company to use its best endeavours to bring this to pass. The Company, Mr. Cox was briefly informed, was doing all it could.

The Commissioners meanwhile burrowed away and November 1876 saw the Commission's "Revised Draft". Again it failed to accede to the Company's prime plea. Funds for a new school, however, should

21

now be found more rapidly; not from the vaguely specified unapplied surplus accumulations of Tonbridge School's Judd funds, but through the sum of £1,000 annually to be set aside from those funds, togetherwith the Hunt and Atwell funds previously on offer. Both in Tonbridge and Tunbridge Wells men took heart. More so perhaps in the latter town. For the location of the new school, as the Revised Draft defined it, should be "within the parish of Tonbridge or within a distance of 10 miles by the ordinary roads or ways from the church of the said town of Tonbridge". Surely these limits must have had Tunbridge Wells in mind. The events of the next decade were casting their shadows before them.

The stage was now set for the final confrontation:

Could the Company raise its bid yet further to retain its unfettered governing power?

Could it indeed, as the Commissioners persisted, supplement its Hunt and Atwell funds' surplus by a substantial sum drawn from its own coffers?

Many would have broken off negotiations with the Commission forthwith and again have resigned from their management of Sir Andrew Judd's foundation, rather than yield to intolerable pressure. The majority opinion nonetheless was to go the other mile.

After lengthy debate as the old year drew to its close, the Court of the Company took the decisive step on 2nd January 1877. It would provide £10,000 from its own corporate funds, which together with the Hunt and Atwell moneys would yield £20,000 for a new school's beginning. Two days later this crucial decision was conveyed to yet another deputation from Tonbridge. Confident, as it was, that in return for its continued support of the Company's cherished prerogative, the new school would ultimately be sited within its town's borders, the deputation expressed wholehearted satisfaction with what was now proposed. It would continue independently to promote the Company's views. It would hope in time to receive its due reward.

This time the Commissioners too were content. They took their time, but pressed on with their task. Their newly revised "Draft for Consideration", dated 11th July 1877, embodied the Company's generous proposals. On handing over the sum of £10,000 from their own funds, the Skinners should remain sole governors both of their present and of their future school. Nor would the Judd funds of the former, be called upon for the new foundation. The Battle of the Scheme had been fought and was now all but won. The Commissioners at least could be pardoned, if they thought so. The Battle of the Site had yet to come.

Within Tonbridge School itself, a note of profound relief was understandably struck forthwith. At its Skinners' Day celebrations a fortnight after the new proposal's date, when the Court of the Skinners' Company paid its annual Visitation, both the Headmaster, the Rev. Theophilus B. Rowe and the Master of the Company, Mr. R. K. Causton, could welcome with delight the latest proposals, received as they had been by the Company that very morning. Some of the governors indeed had as yet had no time to read them. Only a few nights earlier, the persistent M.P. for Rochester, Mr. Julian Goldsmid, had again raised in the Commons the delay in publishing the new School Scheme. But now in the light of the Master's long awaited word, all must surely be plain sailing. The Headmaster could now press ahead with reform of his school's curriculum, boarding and other arrangements.

Meanwhile he could happily join the Tonbridge townsmen present in offering the warmest thanks to the Company for its generous resolution of recent controversy and pay his tribute to the Company's good government of his school in past years. As to the new foundation, he observed, the sum proffered by the Company was enough to make a "fair and good school". Some boys might even leave the old school for the new, nor would he resist this. Should they do so, however, they would only be "on the modern side". Classicists, we are reminded, still reigned supreme. As to the future, he anticipated no great success for the new school at the outset, but added in magnanimous vein, if the press reported him verbatim, that it might well slowly rise until it "equalled the old school in efficiency and perhaps beat it".

It remained to tidy up the scheme's final draft — or more correctly, drafts. For February 1878 saw the promulgation of twin schemes, upon which observations, or objections, were invited within the duly prescribed time. Scheme no. 252 "in the matter of the Foundation known as the Free Grammar School of Sir Andrew Judd" concerned the administration of the long established school. Scheme no.253 "in the matter of the Skinners' Companies' Charities- those of Thomas Hunt and Lawrence Atwell in particular - made provision for the establishment of "a Second Grade School to be called the Skinners' Company's Middle School". Its siting, we note, now "in or near the parish of Tonbridge."

Even now, however, a note of mild mistrust might be heard from the Commissioners' corner. The two schemes must proceed pari passu — in step. Reforms in the internal affairs of Tonbridge School must await the formal acceptance by all concerned, and Her Majesty's ultimate approval of both schemes. The Company must moreover hand over its own £10,000 first. Scheme No. 252 (the Tonbridge School Scheme) should not become law until one day after Scheme No. 253.

If the main issues, moreover, were resolved, much discussion — and two more years — must be fulfilled before Her Majesty in Council would be graciously pleased to declare her approval of both schemes. Public debate meanwhile continued unabated, both Tonbridge and Tunbridge Wells committees actively vigilant and determined. If at times the Tonbridge committee and other Tonbridge spokesmen expressed reservations or raised formal objections, as for instance did the Headmaster and his colleagues, as to features of the Tonbridge School scheme affecting their more local interests, the committee continued resolute as ever regarding the new school's siting.

There were indeed reasons enough for continuing controversy and delay within Tonbridge, especially regarding the new Tonbridge School Scheme. Not all Tonbridge residents were as concerned for a new school as for the protection of local residents' privileges in the matter of fees and university awards. If the attractions of local residence were so diminished as to discourage strangers from seeking houses within the town to enable their sons to attend Tonbridge School, would not the bottom fall out of the housing market, leaving a host of unsaleable properties and catastrophic loss to tradesmen too?

Even His Grace the Archbishop of Canterbury also felt impelled to register his complaint with the Commissioners, regretting that the latest draft proposals no longer named him with his successors as Visitor to Tonbridge School, according that honour to Her Majesty in Council in future years. Yet in the event of differences arising between Tonbridge School Chapel and Tonbridge Parish Church, how could any other than an Archbishop rule between the two parties?

The Company indeed thanked the Archbishop for his observations, whilst diplomatically accepting Mr. Rowe's suggestion that, as the Archbishop was Visitor to All Souls College, Oxford, if the school should ever seek the college's advice, as the school's existing statutes already permitted, the Archbishop might still effectively, if indirectly, fulfil the Visitor's function to the school too.

Lobbying in the meantime by both Tonbridge and Tunbridge Wells continued determinedly. The smaller township of Southborough midway between the prime contestants saw fit to enter its own claims too, the Southborough Local Board pressing the claims of a site in the vicinity of Christ Church, Holden Park, offered by Mr. P. Woolley. The violent indignation with which the versatile Mr. Blair of the Tonbridge Free Press, increasingly the champion of his adopted town's claims, deprecates Southborough's intrusion into the two team contest makes most interesting reading. "Probably there are plenty of landowners in places where building is overdone, and land is a drag on the market, who would be glad to give three or four acres to raise enormously the value of their remaining acres. We have seen a sprat used to catch a mackerel".

Inevitably the euphoria of mid-1877, when the Company's generous offer of its own corporate funds cut the Gordian Knot, faded as time elapsed and no firm schemes finally resolved all issues. In Tonbridge town the implications of the latest draft's phrasing — in, or near, the *parish* of Tonbridge — exercised the minds increasingly as the months passed, whatever men's confidence in the town's agreement, as they believed it to be, in earlier years with the Skinners' Company.

Whether by letter, deputation to the Company or representation direct to the Commissioners, Mr. Homersham Cox and his companions left no stone whatsoever unturned in their efforts to expunge the offensive phrase by something more exclusive. An alternative expression "within the Local Board District of Tonbridge" was vigorously canvassed, whilst persistent reference was made to the several occasions on which the Company had spoken of a school "at Tonbridge" or of the "Tonbridge Middle Class School".

Closer examination of the small print, as it were, of the draft scheme No. 253 gave the Tonbridge party yet further food for anxious thought.

Did not the present proposals suggest a school of somewhat higher standing than the town's tradesmen demanded or required?

Should not the leaving age be set at 15 rather than 17, leaving three or four years at the existing school for outstanding scholars to build upon foundations soundly implanted in the lower grade school?

Should not the curriculum proposals lay more stress on commercial subjects — book-keeping, mensuration and other such practical considerations?

Might there not even be a danger, if the new school's aims and objects were not much more drastically restricted, that it could rival the Company's present school?

Surely this had never been the Would-be donors' intentions?
Could the Commissioners all along have had in mind a school in Tunbridge Wells, where that more fashionable community's influential residents might conceivably nurture a school which in due course might pose comparison with its distinguished forebear?
Despite the Company's capitulation in early 1877 the battle, sadly, still raged. Those primarily concerned with reformation of the ancient grammar school must often have been irked by the persistence of fellow townsmen, whose unwearying pressure regarding the new foundation, accompanied as it so often was by scathing condemnation of the Skinners' Company's seeming breach of faith, inevitably delayed the fulfilment of their own cherished plans. The governors would, however, make their visitation to the old school three times more before the twin schemes became legally binding on all concerned.

Mr. Cox and his fellow townsmen in the meantime received little encouragement in December 1878 in the Commissioners' reply to their own memorial despatched in the previous May. Briefly, the Commissioners "thought it not expedient" to narrow the limits within which the new school was to be placed. They understood, as they added, that the Skinners' Company concurred in this opinion. Whether or not this could fairly be said at this stage, must certainly be questioned to judge from the Company's own records.

Two further points in the Commissioners' response, however, were certainly relevant.

The charities now scheduled to fund a Middle School's establishment were not local Tonbridge funds, as were the Judd Foundation's.

The likely effect, too, of prejudging the new school's siting would be to raise the price of the land to be bought.

Tunbridge Wells once more took heart. As 1879 proceeded it slowly became evident that the final schemes were virtually signed and sealed. Petitions, memorials, lobbying of whatever kind could do no more. Mr. Blair's frenzied representations, righteous indignation and clarion calls to pursue the fight further could no longer avail. By June 1879, the Commissioners were able to inform the Skinners' Company that the Scheme for a Middle School "in or near the parish of Tonbridge" had been duly approved by the Commission — alongside its companion scheme — and submitted to Her Majesty's Education Council.

In the fullness of time, having lain for the statutory two months on the table of the House of Commons, both schemes duly appeared, approved by Her Majesty in Council at the Court at Osborne House, Isle of Wight, and both dated the 31st July, 1880. The two schemes married to the last, we note the final clause of Tonbridge School's own scheme, that its date "shall be the day on which Her Majesty declares her approbation of this scheme, or of the said scheme framed by the Charity Commissioners for the administration of the Skinners' Company's Middle School, whichever day shall last happen".

The Commissioners' wheels had ground slowly.

To many involved in the two towns, they must already have seemed to have ground exceeding small.

CHAPTER 3

THE FIGHT FOR THE SITE

There had inevitably been speculation for some years, both in Tonbridge and Tunbridge Wells, as to appropriate sites for the Company's new school. The Revised Draft Scheme's encouragement spurred Tunbridge Wells especially to renewed endeavour, to assert its rights as within the parish of Tonbridge. In evident belief that the Commissioners were pressing the Company towards Tunbridge Wells, Mr. W. F. Browell, increasingly the leader in his town's campaign, had already in April 1878 challenged his fellow townsmen to raise such a sum, by public subscription, as would enable his town to purchase an adequate site for the reception of the Company's gift.

Mr. & Mrs. T. Jones-Gibb

Within weeks, the monthly meeting of the Town's Tradesmen's Association had enthusiastically volunteered "upwards of 250 guineas" from among its several members. July saw both the Courier's and the Gazette's publication of a near-column length Subscription List, totalling around £1,500. A most generous promise of £500 headed the list under the names of T. Jones-Gibbs Esq. and Mrs. Jones- Gibbs, with the Appeal Committee's Chairman, the Honourable F. G. Molyneux donating £100 and the Rev. Canon Hoare, Trinity Parsonage, £20. A note appended to the list over the Chairman's name and those of W. F. Browell (Corresponding Secretary) and F. Argyle (Minute Secretary) stressed the committee's aim to raise £4,000, which should be "an additional argument of such weight as to turn the scale in favour of this town".

The initial success of this Subscription List seemed certainly a serious threat to Tonbridge, provoking that town's Free Press to accuse Tunbridge Wells of seeking to bribe the Company by the offer of a site. If so much could be forthcoming so quickly, was not this a sign that the town was rich enough to endow its own school without outside help?

Not so, of course, as Mr. R. Pelton, bookseller upon the Pantiles,

painstakingly replied in the next edition of his own town's journal. Did not the Skinners' Company now see that Tonbridge already had its own school, whereas Tunbridge Wells had no adequate institution for the schooling of its substantial middle classes? Nor was it, as Mr. Pelton proceeded, "essentially a tradesmen's question", to quote Mr Homersham Cox. The new school should serve a much wider clientele than that of tradesmen only. The Tunbridge Wells Subscription List moved steadily, if slowly, upwards in succeeding weeks. The Tonbridge committee likewise expressed its intention to present its own site to the Company. Sites at Primrose Hill

Mr. Richard Pelton

(today's Hastings Road), Brook Street and Quarry Hill were actively debated and their virtues sung in anxious representations to the Court of the Company.

Meanwhile, a speech to the Tunbridge Wells Tradesmen's Association's Annual Dinner in November 1878 threatened to put a new complexion upon the whole affair. In replying to the toast of the Visitors, Mr. Edward Cazalet, of Fairlawn, Shipbourne, declared his own belief that the essential reason for the woefully small number of tradesmen's sons in Tonbridge School was the highly classical nature of that school, which gave an education most unsuitable to their needs. Tonbridge, he believed, was making a great mistake in accepting the sop of a new school "I have said to Sir Seymour Fitzgerald, the Chief Commissioner", he proceeded, "that what we want is a modern school.... and such a modern school should be grafted on to Tonbridge School". Moreover Tonbridge and Tunbridge Wells should stop wrangling and press together to put Sir Andrew Judd's existing school on a more satisfactory footing.

Mr. Cazalet's words were received, as the press reported, "with cheers". On such a convivial occasion in vino, there might well have been veritas. Good-will and friendship might yet have prevailed between the rival towns. It was not, however, to be. Seizing primarily upon Mr. Cazalet's suggestion in the same speech that one hundred, say, Tonbridge tradesmen's sons paying total fees of £1,500 per annum would yield insufficient income to support a separate new school, Mr. Browell leapt to the defence of his own town's claim in the next issue of his local press. The much larger town with its far greater complement of professional and business men was in a far better position, he urged, to support a new foundation. It could offer, moreover, a choice of admirable sites and was plainly willing to add a large sum to the £20,000 promised by the Company. Men of Tonbridge meanwhile should indeed take Mr. Cazalet's words to heart. Let them see, before it was too late, the poor prospects of a Middle School within their smaller town.

Failing to reconcile the two townships and to prevent their parallel pressures for a new and separate school, Mr. Cazalet subsequently made a direct offer of £10,000 to Tonbridge School to establish a modern department within the existing school. Sadly, however, Mr. Cazalet's offer was not to be fulfilled. Before details of his project could be agreed, he died unexpectedly a few years later on a visit to Constantinople. News of his offer, indeed, momentarily persuaded Tunbridge Wells that a decision had been taken to site the new school in Tunbridge Wells. Mr. Cazalet, however, quickly denied that any such intention was implicit in his offer. Controversy continued, nothing was resolved.

If the door indeed remained open for the new school's location in Tunbridge Wells, Messrs. Cox, Blair and companions were resolute and resourceful as ever. Much water must still flood the Medway's stream before either town's hopes could become fact. It was true that opinion within the Skinners' Company appeared substantially in favour of Tonbridge. It voted indeed in November 1880 to accept the offer of a Tonbridge site, limiting the Company's commitment to a school of 100 boys only in the first instance, with buildings so constructed, however, as to permit extension to accommodate more day boys and a limited number of boarders, if thought desirable later.

For whatever reason, this decision in favour of Tonbridge was rescinded in the following month. The Company may well have been made more clearly aware of the Commissioners' views in the intervening weeks. A more cautious resolution prevailed that further discussion be sought with the Commissioners, in which the claims not only of Tonbridge but also of Tunbridge Wells and other places within the parish of Tonbridge might be more fully considered. Consideration was at the same meeting deferred of an eagerly optimistic letter from Mr. Pelton of Tunbridge Wells, forwarding a memorial from his townsmen requesting the Company to engage a temporary building in Tunbridge Wells and to open their school forthwith. A further letter from Mr. A. Nicholson, enclosing a map of Tunbridge Wells showing the parts of the town, from which scholars might be expected to be drawn, was likewise set aside for future examination.

Beset as the Company was by pressures on every side, it was in no way surprising that Mr. Homersham Cox's request for yet another deputation to address the Court of the Company in December 1880 was parried with a request that his views be presented this time in writing. Fervent representation from "inhabitants residing on the South side of Tonbridge" and from "250 resident householders of Tonbridge", as also a memorial from the Tonbridge Local Board were equally referred to a smaller sub-committee for further consideration.

It must be accepted that further consideration in Victorian days was leisurely indeed. Little appears to have surfaced throughout 1881, whether for good or ill, for Tonbridge or for Tunbridge Wells. There were those indeed in Tunbridge Wells, quietly confident perhaps of ultimate victory in the boys' school battle, who were turning their attention to a parallel cause, that of schooling for middle class girls.

A public meeting in the Great Hall, Tunbridge Wells, in August 1881, again with the Honourable F. G. Molyneux in the chair, readily yielded a provisional committee charged with the establishment of a High School for Girls under the auspices of the influential Girls Public Day School Trust. If this new committee had in mind to shame those working so slowly in pursuit of the boys' school, they must be allowed to have succeeded. Tunbridge Wells High School for Girls duly opened its doors at Fairlawn, Mount Sion, early in 1883. The Middle Grade School for Girls had also come to birth in a schoolroom attached to Emmanuel Church through the efforts of its minister, the Rev.

George Jones. From the latter of these two girls' schools sprang in due time the Tunbridge Wells Girls Grammar School of today. The High School sadly slipped from the scene in the difficult days of the Second World War.

The Great Hall, Tunbridge Wells

Meanwhile, however little stirred on the surface, plainly much unreported discussion ensued behind the scenes. A majority within the Skinners' Company would doubtless have still been happy to site their new school in Tonbridge to honour the undertaking given, however loosely, in an earlier year, in return for that town's support for the Company's unchanged government of its earlier cherished foundation.

A perusal today of the Company's minute books makes it plain indeed that, as 1881 moved on its way, the Company's opinion hardened in favour of the grimly named Bloodshot site at Primrose Hill on the Hastings Road, the property of the Goldsmid family trustees. The Company were happy, too, to communicate their intentions in writing to Mr. Blair. For a moment in June Mr. Blair's press felt able to indulge in unreserved rejoicing. With all possible relief and delight he could share with his fellow townsmen the "gratifying intelligence" that his committee's efforts had at length been crowned with complete success. Sadly, however, for Tonbridge the news was premature — and false. The Commissioners would have the last word. They pressed steadfastly, as we must conclude, for Tunbridge Wells.

Mr. E. H. Strange

Little word of this relatively gentlemanly confrontation stirred either town for many months. More than a twelvemonth passed before the Tunbridge Wells Tradesmens' Association is again reported in September 1881 to have reviewed the situation. Once again by unanimous decision the tradesmen resolved to despatch their plea to the Commissioners, with copies thereof to the Prime Minister and Attorney General. As yet, we note, no clear word of any bargain between the Company and the Tonbridge Committee seems to have reached Tunbridge Wells' ears. It could scarcely remain undisclosed for long.

It was not, however, until early March 1882 that his local news sheets reported Mr. Strange's revelation to the Tunbridge Wells Local Board of his understanding that the Skinners' Company had made a promise to the residents of Tonbridge to site the new school in their town in return for their support on the governing body issue. Mr. Browell too spoke vigorously of his indignation at "what he must consider an incautious promise to the Tonbridge people", despite which, as he insisted, the Company had continued to negotiate with the Tunbridge Wells committee, treating the issue, as he had believed, as a completely open matter between the two towns. Open, too, he stressed it still was in the terms of the published scheme's wording "in or near the parish". He had accordingly requested the Commissioners to receive a Tunbridge Wells deputation before taking its site decision. This, he understood, the Commissioners were willing to do. Meanwhile he again expressed his serious doubt as to the rival town's ability to provide a suitable site and adequate financial support.

The gloves indeed were finally off. Perfidious Tonbridge stood revealed!

Perfidious Skinners presumably too! Once again, Tunbridge Wells' press paraded its lengthy Subscription List of those willing to assist the new school's siting in Tunbridge Wells. An attendant note, moreover, stressed almost stridently the urgent need for both action and funds. "After a long delay and great fluctuation", as the note proceeded, the Company had seemed in the last year to have decided against the claims of Tunbridge Wells and Southborough. An admirable site in Tunbridge Wells had, however, been indicated and a large sum promised. The committee indeed had every reason to believe that these considerations would have had their proper weight but for some "incautious promises made a long time ago, of which the committee knew nothing till last summer". The approval, though, of the Charity Commissioners had not yet been given. A deputation had yet to be heard ... promises of abundant financial support could yet save the day.

For whatever reason, the Tunbridge Wells deputation was unable to meet the Commissioners until mid July 1882. The Tunbridge Wells Local Board had meanwhile held its Annual General Meeting in May, when Mr. Argyle told of his call at the Commissioners' office in London a few days previously. The Skinners' Company, he was told, had indeed submitted to the Commissioners a firm proposal to site the new school in Tonbridge. He had received an assurance none the less that no decision in the matter would be taken before the Tunbridge Wells deputation had been heard.

Two months later it was so heard, and the report of its discussion duly made to its town. Briefly, as Mr. Browell reported, the Chairman of the Charity Commissioners had instanced one circumstance, and one circumstance only, which in the Commissioners' view gave Tonbridge any advantage over Tunbridge Wells. Tonbridge had offered a site free of cost. Tunbridge Wells could only with certainty offer a field of 11 acres, much larger than was required, and a sum insufficient for that field's purchase. Towards the present purchase price of £4,750 the Subscription List to date mustered about £2,000.

The Commissioners, however, gave Tunbridge Wells fourteen days in which to put itself in the same position as Tonbridge. It was the deputation's view that Mr. Hopwood, the owner of the field, should be asked to sell sufficient land, say 5-6 acres, next to the High Road (St. John's Road, as we today know it), at a proportionate reduction in price; and that steps be taken to ensure such land's purchase. In Mr. Browell's submission, the Commissioners had virtually admitted that in every other respect Tunbridge Wells' claims were superior to its rival's.

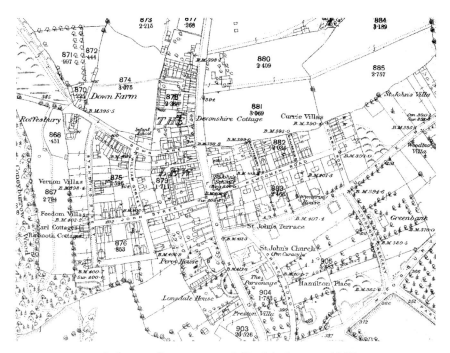

Ordnance Survey map of St. John's area, 1867

The challenge to the town was now crystal clear. More money must be assured forthwith. In any case the current list's total must be regarded with caution. As yet it was primarily of promises rather than money received. Some subscribers had died, since the list first opened, or had moved elsewhere. Hard cash was now called for, and notwithstanding the claims of a rival site at Mount Sion, canvassed at the same meeting, the Local Board members present voted with enthusiasm for urgent efforts to secure the necessary portion of Mr. Hopwood's field, so well sited, as Mr. Browell observed being only 125 yards from Queen's Road "one of the most popular parts of the town". Significantly the report of the Local Board's meeting concluded by expressing belief that Mr. Hopwood was willing to sell the smaller area of land required.

A representative of the Commissioners had indeed recently paid a visit to both towns' proffered sites. It was generally anticipated that a decision was imminent. Whistling perhaps to keep his spirits up, Mr. Blair in Tonbridge, looking at the merits of the two towns' cases, could be in no doubt, as he affirmed that the verdict would be in Tonbridge's favour, since "all considerations of justice and expediency lead in the same direction". Meanwhile his Tunbridge Wells Courier

35

counterpart paraded his wholehearted support for his townsmen, whilst philosophizing gently regarding the present state of play in their long drawn engagement with the neighbouring 'town of bridges".

Whereas Tonbridge, he mused had for centuries supposedly enjoyed the benefits of Tonbridge School, its bona fide citizens seemed not to have benefited from the school either directly or indirectly, inasmuch as they had allowed their birthright to glide away to impecunious strangers. These outsiders, seeking residence in Tonbridge sufficient to qualify their sons for a share in the benefits of Sir Andrew Judd's Foundation, had usurped the rights of the natives. In the circumstances, it was not to be wondered at, that men of Tonbridge were making zealous efforts to secure a new school of their own. Nor could it be gainsaid that in the recent past by their vigorous representation and in particular by their compact with the Skinners' Company, they might be thought to be virtually masters of the field. The Charity Commissioners could nonetheless even at this late hour veto their well laid plans. It remained for the "fashionable metropolis of Kent" to say whether it would provide the necessary funds to frustrate its neighbour's knavish tricks, or whether Tonbridge should have it all its own way. The Tunbridge Wells site now proposed could serve Southborough well too. Let Tunbridge Wells and Southborough be now but true to themselves. In a fortnight all could be changed.

For some weeks beyond the fortnight deadline, the Subscription List, regularly republished and week by week modestly revised, bore mounting tribute to the local committee's efforts. Its members' eloquence, too, made itself heard in gatherings of all descriptions, as when Mr. Argyle addressed a Special Meeting of the Tunbridge Wells Farmers' Club a few days later. Mr Langdell's proposal that the club should contribute 10 guineas to the Middle School Fund had required a special meeting to approve or reject the proposition. Nor did Mr Argyle fail to persuade his farmer friends to put their shoulders to his wheel. Let tradesmen and farmers combine to fill the new school and to keep the "foreign element" out. Tunbridge Wells must not fall into the same groove as Tonbridge.

Once again, the familiar complaints were aired of the supposedly generous provision now offered to the working classes' children and of the "upper ten looking after themselves". The deserving middle classes — and on this occasion the farmers — were alone overlooked. We may smile at Farmer Roper's observation that the lower classes indeed "got the best of it". He knew this as an indisputable fact from what he had seen at Frant National School. After he had been at Tonbridge School for five years, he would have been ashamed to show his handwriting against boys of 10 or 12 at Frant!

Meanwhile it became increasingly evident that the Skinners' Company was indeed no longer a free agent. At the opening of the Tonbridge Free Library in July 1882, Mr. Cazalet, not yet embarked on his fatal visit to interview the Sultan, referred openly to his concern at this fact and deplored the Commissioners' involvement in the town's affairs. Nor was it wholly surprising that readers of its edition of 1st September found the Tunbridge Wells Courier reporting "on reliable authority" that the Charity Commissioners had declined to sanction the site offered by the Tonbridge committee and that a formal word to this effect had already been received in Tonbridge.

No similar communication, however, it was admitted had as yet been addressed to their Tunbridge Wells rivals. For a few days, possibly weeks, doubts as to the true facts lingered. The Tonbridge Free Press flatly contradicted its contemporary's statement. By early October, however, it could no longer be denied, however much Mr. Homersham Cox and his companions were disposed to dispute it.

Nor was debate confined within the two town's borders, when the furious Mr. Cox expressed his dismay and indignation in a forthright letter to The Times. He bitterly attacked the Commissioners for their change of front, as he expressed it, at the eleventh hour. In consequence of this the Skinners' Company had been compelled to renege upon its word. Inevitably the rival case was at once presented to The Times' readers, when Mr. Browell in his turn begged to expose "the fundamental error pervading every line of Mr. Cox's letter", insisting that Tonbridge town had no greater claim on Sir Andrew Judd's foundation than Tunbridge Wells or Southborough, and that "in or near the parish" most certainly was intended to embrace a far wider tract than Tonbridge town alone. Nor could the Company's vote in favour of Tonbridge "after many years' hesitation" be accepted as the last word. That lay plainly with the Commissioners, who would take account of the relative population figures and would "naturally" consider that the school would be more useful in Tunbridge Wells.

Feeling ran high indeed in Tonbridge, and found expression in unlikely places, as in Mr. T. L. Devitt's reported speech at a Rearing Feast in Tonbridge to celebrate completion of a house built for him at Godden Green by Messrs. Punnett and Son. In proposing the health of the two foremen involved, Mr. Devitt, a Warden at the time of the Skinners' Company, scathingly attacked the Commissioners and expressed his earnest hope that the new school would still be built in Tonbridge, and that it would soon be his good fortune, as the Company's Master, as we may surmise, to be working again with Messrs. Punnett. Mr. E. Punnett's subsequent observation that he hoped "they would kick against the school going to Tunbridge Wells" reads as a somewhat muted version of what was doubtless more forcibly expressed in many quarters.

Not that it was clear in the closing months of 1882 that the Tunbridge Wells site, whose purchase price had been so urgently called for within two short weeks, was necessarily to be the one finally chosen. Rumour was also rife that Sir David Lionel Salomons, Bart, had offered a site on his own estate to the Tunbridge Wells committee — at a reasonable price, too, as the local press observed, and certainly less than the honourable baronet paid for it. He was declared furthermore to have promised £1,000, when the school's foundation stone was laid. Nothing more, however, was heard in the months following of this mooted offer.

The Skinners' Company meanwhile continued to ponder how best it could even yet honour its pledge to its friends in Tonbridge and, even at this stage, circumvent the Commissioners' intransigence. Whatever the final decision, its members knew all too well that they must in any case incur the wrath of one or other party. At length, however, the Master, Clerk and other members of the Company ventured forth on the last day of February, 1883, to meet the Tunbridge Wells committee on its site "on the Lew', as its natives generally knew it. There Messrs. W. F. Browell, T. F. Simpson, G. Cheverton, F. Argyle and A. Nicholson delighted to meet the Company's party, as it arrived in open carriages, as we read, from Tonbridge shortly before 3 o'clock.

What the reception party seem not to have known is that the Company's representatives had earlier in the day met the Tonbridge committee and examined the Quarry Hill site owned by the same Mr. Punnett, the builder. Indeed at the end of the day, as the Company's records tell, the Company's preference remained for the Quarry Hill site. Strangely no hint of the day's earlier visit appears in either town's journals. That no word surfaced of the Company's initial reaction, is perhaps more understandable in a sensitive situation.

Be that as it may, Mr. Browell presented his case with the aid of plans and further information afforded by Mr. Peter Dodd, the town's assistant surveyor. The Company's representatives shrewdly refrained from comment whilst expressing their warmest thanks to Mr. Browell and his friends. That the site could be handed over without delay being readily confirmed, the carriages were soon on their way down Mount Pleasant to the South Eastern Railway Station and its train back to town.

Tunbridge Wells' hopes ran high. Mr. Browell could express quiet confidence, when the Second Grade School's question was yet again raised at the Local Board's meeting a few days later. Nor could he agree with Mr. Clifford, whose regularly repetitive question would become a feature of the Board's proceedings for many months to come, that a more determined approach should be made to the Company forthwith to ensure a successful conclusion to Tunbridge Wells' endeavours. Let things be allowed to run a little longer as they were.

The tide was running Tunbridge Wells way. Meanwhile the town's Tradesmen's Association's annual report recorded the association's vote of ten guineas towards the site subscription fund, to supplement the generous sums subscribed by individual members.

Not for a moment, however, could anyone have expected Tonbridge to acknowledge defeat. Yet again the clarion call to Public Meeting went forth from Messrs. Cox and Blair. Nor were words minced in the notice of this occasion. Before March 1883 had run its course, men of Tonbridge were urgently facing the fact, as the meeting's callers averred, that "whereas the Skinners' Company were desirous of placing the new school near Tonbridge Railway Station, the Charity Commissioners were endeavouring to compel them to adopt a site at Tunbridge Wells".

There was no lack of eloquent and influential spokesmen to plead the Tonbridge case. The Headmaster of Tonbridge School, unable to be present in person, in his written submission cogently summarised the townsmen's grievances whilst openly accepting in disarming fashion his school's detachment from the community around it. "Owing to natural and necessary developments in education, the school is educating less than a dozen natives and only three belonging to the trading classes. The new scheme of 31st July 1880 recognises and perpetuates this for the future... and deprives the town definitely of all chances of such an education as the mass of the inhabitants require". When the Company had envisaged a new school in 1870 in Tonbridge or some adjacent locality, no one could have envisaged Tunbridge Wells as an adjacent locality. Had not the Company's Clerk's letter to the Tonbridge deputation of 14th October 1875 also spoken specifically of a new school "at Tonbridge"? The Commissioner's own Draft Scheme of 1875 had used the phrase "in or near the town of Tonbridge". It had only been in 1877 that such phrases as "within the parish" or "within ten miles of Tonbridge Parish Church" had been insinuated into the discussions. The men of Tonbridge had been outrageously affronted and wantonly deceived. The Commissioners' actions could not have been more high-handed.

There followed a rousing speech by Mr. Homersham Cox. Fifty years ago, when he had attended Tonbridge School, there had been no difference between gentlemen's and tradesmen's sons. But today... little by little the school had lost that character and become chiefly for the upper classes. The Skinners' Company now sought to make amends, and no Charity Commissioner should stand in its path. Nor had Tunbridge Wells any possible claim on the Company's benevolence. Only in the last few years had that town shown any interest whatsoever in the area's educational provision.

Mr. G. D. Warner's resolution, that the "earnest thanks of the inhabitants of Tonbridge are due to the Skinners' Company for their munificent endowment of a Second Grade School and for their continued determination to establish it at Tonbridge", was unanimously approved. As also was a further resolution that a petition be presented to Parliament and a memorial despatched to the Education Department, praying that the Company's decision to establish the new school at Tonbridge be carried into effect forthwith.

That the Skinners' Company was the innocent victim of the Commissioners' malevolence was common ground throughout an indignant meeting. As a distinguished Past Master of the Company resident in the locality, Mr. J. F. Wadmore, observed, speaking as an individual, the Company felt itself under the threats of the Commissioners, who could sweep it away altogether. This was indeed an age for the "removal of landmarks", and however much the Company's members sympathised with the town's aspirations, as he did himself most warmly, their views had been over-ridden in a most tyrannical manner.

Nor could Mr. Blair's reading to the meeting, presumably with the Company's approval, of the last clause of a "very strong" letter sent by the Company to the Commissioners three days before Christmas 1882 — regretting that it was not in a position to find money for a school in Tunbridge Wells and that it would be sorry if Tonbridge did not primarily derive benefit from the funds forming the capital investment of the proposed Middle School — have wholly removed concern and apprehension from the staunchest of Tonbridge breasts. As the meeting drew to its end, the Chairman might well seek to rally his troops by his fervent hope that the Commissioners would be persuaded to prepare yet another scheme, which would require to be presented afresh to the Education Department, with which, as he confidently asserted, they were "practically safe". But were they? And would the Commissioners so readily oblige?

Arms of the Skinners' Company

At this stage Tunbridge Wells had not the least thought of withdrawal. Within days of his local print's lengthy account of the Tonbridge meeting, Mr. Browell's pen leapt yet again to paper. The old familiar arguments were once again paraded in the Courier pages. Precisely the same grievances, he maintained, as to exclusion from the benefits of Sir Andrew's foundation, were felt by Tunbridge Wells and Southborough tradesmen as by their fellows in Tonbridge; that many members of the Skinners' Company appreciated Tunbridge Wells' claims, as was supported by the most courteous correspondence.

between the Company and the local committee; that the Commissioners were patently seized of the virtues of Tunbridge Wells' admirable site in an open, airy part of the town — and in the parish of Tonbridge; that the likelihood of Parliamentary interference was minimal. He had every hope that the town would soon hear that its site was accepted.

So too his Town's Local Board was fully confident of imminent success. Meanwhile Mr. Clifford in particular kept his fellow members on their toes — by question, criticism or occasional jibe. Was it not true that their Tonbridgian counterparts were far more active than they were themselves? Apart from Mr. Browell s recent letter, what else had been done to assert their legitimate claims? To which, one at least of his fellows was prompted to ask in reply, "Why should not Mr. Clifford be added to the town's school committee?" Some of his sting might well have been drawn, if nothing more.

Inevitably Mr. Browell's contribution to the Courier pages drew its riposte from none other than Mr. Blair himself, sole editor, manager, reporter, compositor, indeed founder and owner of his Tonbridge Free Press. Was it not clear to every unprejudiced mind, he asked his rival's readers, that Tunbridge Wells was non-existent, when Sir Andrew made his bequest? What hurt had Tonbridge School's new scheme inflicted on Tunbridge Wells in any way comparable with the losses sustained by Tonbridge? Did not Tunbridge Wells already possess a number of adequate private schools, which would still suffice, if the new school were built in Tonbridge? Mr Browell and his friends were seeking to do Tonbridge an injury such as none of them individually would for a moment think of doing to a neighbour.

The Tunbridge Wells Local Board's monthly meetings — and Mr. Clifford's persistence — certainly ensured that interest never flagged. If nothing yet had been heard from either Commissioners or Company, as Mr. Browell patiently replied to Mr. Clifford at the May 1883 meeting, he had nonetheless been greatly encouraged by the Southborough Local Board's recent expression of its strong desire that the question should be settled by the school being sited in Tunbridge Wells. He was aware indeed of disagreement within the Skinners' ranks. If this could not be resolved, the question might well arise whether there should be a new school at all, not where it should be sited. He had reason nonetheless to believe that the Commissioners continued unwilling to approve a Tonbridge site. A courteous letter to the Company urging an early decision might perhaps be helpful.

Replies were still awaited from both Commissioners and Company at the Board's next meeting in June, as Mr. Clifford's "standing question" quickly revealed. July 1883, however, finally brought the long awaited word. The Skinners' Company "were willing to negotiate with the Tunbridge Wells committee relative to the site at St John's Road". The matter, Mr. Browell moved, should be referred at once to the board's oddly named Duties of Officers Committee. Most of the work had already been done by his committee, which had already written to the landowner's solicitor asking that he would communicate at once with the Skinners' Company. £3,000 would now be called for very soon. The greater part of this was already promised. May these promises now, please, be converted into cash.

What might have been:
Sir David Lionel Salomons Bt.
rumoured to have offered a site for the School
on his Broomfield Estate at Southborough.

CHAPTER 4

THE STRUGGLE CONTINUES

Success at long last, as it seemed, for Tunbridge Wells. All now should proceed without hindrance. In Tonbridge, deep dismay and righteous indignation. His last issue in June 1883 had seen Mr. Blair launch the most blistering attack upon the Commissioners, the manifest villains of the whole wretched business. Every consideration of justice had been ignored by bestowing another body's bounty upon an undeserving town. "Now that all hope of the school being placed at Tonbridge is at an end", as Mr. Blair grudgingly conceded, the rival town, too, suffered his furious verbal assault. The Commissioners, however, bore the brunt of his attack. To quote the somewhat stilted comment of the Tunbridge Wells Courier on reading Mr. Blair's diatribe, they "ought, of course, to find themselves snuffed out".

It was easy to be complacent, when the enemy seemed finally down. Within a few days, moreover, the Skinners' Company's Clerk and Surveyor had visited Tunbridge Wells, being "charmed by the site", as Mr. Brentnall, the Local Board's Surveyor, duly reported to his masters. The town could be happily assured by its faithful press, that negotiations were proceeding favourably for purchase.

If Mr. Clifford could draw no further information in October, November and beyond, there certainly seemed no serious grounds for concern. Mr. Stone-Wigg, a prominent member of the Local Board and destined to become his town's first Mayor, could assure his fellow members in October that he had every hope of an early and successful end to present negotiations, and that the new school would prove "as great a success, as he was told by Mr. Delves, the High School for Girls had been". Nor was Mr. Clifford likely to have been unduly dismayed in November, when told that the site had not yet been handed over to the Skinners' Company. That very morning, it was also reported, Mr. Simpson had travelled to London to adjust the contract for the purchase.

As 1884 came in, matters were still thought to be moving forward — slowly perhaps, but surely. The land conveyance was reported to nave been satisfactorily arranged and instructions given to complete the transaction forthwith.

Came March, however, and the Local Board was told that the lawyers were still enquiring into the land's "title". By the following month Mr. Clifford could contain himself no longer. If the chosen site could not be obtained in the very near future, should the committee not be looking for another? Not yet, thought Mr. Browell. The matter, he believed, might still be said to be proceeding. Lawyers were always "apt to dawdle", and there had indeed been delay over title. He was persuaded that the vendors had good title, but were reluctant to show it, as this would involve much expense. The committee had offered to bear this, and very soon this delay should be ended. Meanwhile Mr. Howard, another Board member, was glad to be reassured by Mr. Browell that site subscriptions already received were on deposit at two banks, at 2% and 2½% respectively.

Yet almost two months more passed before word went happily forth that on Thursday, 22nd May, Messrs. Stone, Simpson and Son, acting for the Tunbridge Wells committee, had heard from the Skinners' Company's solicitors that they were satisfied with the site's title, and would forward the contract for signature at once. Surely building must now be very soon started.

Yet, dead though they may have appeared, the men of Tonbridge simply would not lie down. They still had shots in their locker.

On the very day that the Company's confirmatory word was received in Tunbridge Wells, a question was again asked in the House of Commons by Mr. Jesse Collings, the member for Ipswich, palpably at the instigation of Mr. Homersham Cox and his companions. In somewhat tendentious terms Mr. Collings asked Mr. Mundella, Vice President of the Council, if he was aware that Sir Andrew Judd's school at Tonbridge was founded and had been carried on for three centuries as a free school for the benefit of all classes, and that the Charity Commissioners were now insisting on the establishment of a school at Tunbridge Wells, five miles distant, and whether the Government would take steps to restore to the poor and middle classes of Tonbridge their advantages and rights. In reply Mr. Mundella said very succinctly "No". The Charity Commissioners, he thought, had acted wisely. Tunbridge Wells was by far the larger town and within the scope of Sir Andrew's will. To another member of the House, Mr. R. K Causton, whom we met as Master of the Company at Tonbridge

School's Visitation in 1877, who pointed out that the governors had themselves protested unsuccessfully against the changed siting, he replied equally coldly. That was very possible, but such protests did not challenge the rights of the House of Commons.

Tunbridge Wells, when it heard of Mr. Mundella's plain speaking, could certainly take heart. Even more so a few days later, when Mr. Argyle was reported to have made satisfactory arrangements with the site's owners, that the conveyance had been finally settled, and that work would soon begin. It was plainly time for another Town's Meeting to share the good news and, more importantly, to beat the drum to ensure promised subscriptions' actual receipt.

A doubt nonetheless still clouded some Tunbridge Wells minds. There might yet be further lengths to which Tonbridge would go in its implacable opposition to the younger town. Nor had the Tunbridge Wells Tradesmen's Association, it transpired, yet paid its promised ten guineas towards the site's purchase, as that indefatigable enquirer, Mr. Clifford, ascertained, when he questioned the association's treasurer. There were evidently some among the traders, who would only believe in the new school, when it was seen to rise from its foundations.

It was abundantly clear that Mr. Cox would still not let the matter rest, nor can anyone in either town have been surprised when his troops were summoned yet again — to an Indignation Meeting, as the rival town's Courier fairly termed it, in Tonbridge Town Hall at 4 p.m. on Tuesday, 23rd July, 1884. The purpose, as the meeting's notice declared, to protest against the Commissioners' actions and "to consider the expediency of making a fresh application to Parliament on the subject."

It would be tedious, and to little purpose, to report in detail much that was said in a lengthy and lively meeting. Mr. Cox inevitably covered much familiar ground. The Charity Commissioners had prevented the Company's acceptance of a site offered by his town. If what had transpired was not a breach of good faith, then breach of good faith had no meaning in the English language. Referring too to Mr. Collings' recent question in the Commons — a question repeated, it may be noted, only days before the present meeting — he spoke with the utmost scorn of Kent's own MPs, no one of whom, as he asserted, had helped at all. It had been left to a member for an Essex borough to champion the Tonbridge cause. To an outside observer, this might have seemed to suggest that his townsmens' case was less convincing than it appeared in the heated atmosphere of their own Town Hall.

No single dissentient voice was raised, however, when Mr. G. D. Warner proposed his ponderous resolution: that whereas the Commissioners in 1875 proposed that a Second Grade School be established in or near the town of Tonbridge, and whereas after obtaining possession of a sum of £20,000 given by the Skinners Company for that purpose, the Commissioners now insist that the school be placed at Tunbridge Wells, they are guilty of a breach of good faith. Dr. Ievens' proposition that a copy of this resolution be sent to Mr. Mundella with a request that he will use his influence to obtain reconsideration of the Commissioners' decision, was unanimously approved likewise.

As at all times, when men of Tonbridge met in these days, much was said of other things. Despite the conclusion of the new scheme for Tonbridge School itself, some sought to re-open issues already decided. The sharp increase in that school's fees rankled. So too the curtailment of local boys' prior rights, in return for which no compensation was now offered. On every count, it was insisted, pressures improperly applied had conspired to divert the course of natural justice. Sinister influences had somewhere been at work. Mr. West saw the hidden hand of the Marquess of Abergavenny manipulating decisions on Tunbridge Wells' behalf.

Among those concentrating on the Middle, or Second Grade, School issue, two considerations increasingly prevailed; the size of the sum to be made available for its foundation, and the belief that, even if the first battle were irretrievably lost, persistent Tonbridge pressure might even yet yield a second new school in Tonbridge town itself!

Mr. Cox pressed firmly for some part of the £20,000 available to be applied to such a school. The sum to be provided, as he maintained, had steadily advanced, as negotiations proceeded, from £10,000 through £15,000 to the present exceedingly generous figure. As Tonbridge School funds were massively augmented in coming years, Tonbridge might yet hope, whatever the present situation, that some part of the Company's present benefaction might serve as the base from which sufficient funds would accrue to yield a further school. The Commissioners had indeed "done just as much mischief as malignity coupled with ingenuity could accomplish". Sustained pressure might even yet, however, rescue something from the wreckage.

The Vicar of Tonbridge, the Rev. T. Manley, spoke forcefully too. His flock, as he asserted, had been patently ousted from their privileges, having only acquiesced in their loss on the distinct understanding of compensation in the form of a new school of commercial character tailored to the tradesmen's needs. No fair-minded minister surely could rob them of this. A temperate statement of their case to Mr. Mundella might still yield his town a portion of the spoils. So too Mr. Rowe's views, as reported to the meeting, were that, if the townsmen failed at this time to achieve some redress of their "palpable grievances", they would have established a strong moral claim upon his school's mounting revenues in years ahead.

Some of the heart, it might have been thought before the meeting, seemed to have gone out of the Tonbridgians' protest. To many the siting of the new school was a matter substantially decided. As this latest meeting began, no more than half a dozen of the public had been present. As it proceeded, no more than 40 or 50 stirred themselves to attend. As it drew to its end even its Chairman spoke of its despondent tone. But its time, he insisted, had not been thrown away. The interchange of ideas would prove of great value in the future. They were engaged in a good cause, of which they most certainly need not be afraid

Mr. Cox indeed was playing his cards well. There could yet be two winners at the end of the race. Meanwhile, we must observe, in Tunbridge Wells all could scarcely be thought to be well. Negotiations for the site's purchase were moving more slowly than had been believed. To Mr. Clifford's inevitable question at the Local Board's meeting, in August 1884, as to whether the site had been formally handed over, the Chairman could only observe that Mr. Browell was absent and he himself did not know. Mr. Argyle could only add that, although the matter was really "clear as a pikestaff", there remained some question as to the land's identification. It had at one time been called the Old Turnpike Field and there had been a boundary diversion. The Skinners' Company wished — very properly, as he allowed, — to be assured that the land in question was indeed the same as was now offered.

Meanwhile the Tonbridge campaigners sought determinedly to widen their battlefront, to involve all England. Letters to this end were forthwith despatched to the Spectator, to be duly copied in succeeding weeks by the press of both towns. Mr. Rowe's eloquent exposition of his townsmens' complaints was equally lucidly succeeded by Mr. Homersham Cox' further representations and appeal to readers up and down the land. The issue was one, he thundered, of general, not merely local importance. It was high time that public attention should be drawn to the Charity Commissioners' gross abuse of their statutory powers. It was a matter of national importance that a Committee of the House of Commons should investigate their conduct.

As was only to be expected, equally cogent defence of Tunbridge Wells' case came from that town's advocate in the Spectator's next number. Indignantly denying that the Commissioners gained control of £20,000 by stating their intention to spend it within the limited area of Tonbridge town, Mr. Browell reiterated vigorously that the moneys now to be spent derived in no way whatsoever from the Judd funds, upon which the Tonbridge party made such passionate claim, but upon the quite separate Hunt and Atwell Charities and the company's own Corporate Funds.

Venturing, moreover, to return to the Commissioners' abortive proposals of 1875, he referred without hesitation to the "unapplied surplus" of Tonbridge School's Judd funds, which could yet yield its own new school for Tonbridge. For himself, as he piously proceeded, he would be glad to see this fulfilled for his Tonbridge neighbours' benefit, when the accumulations sufficed. Many of the Skinners were in favour of the chosen site in the larger town. The decision now taken had no doubt been a disappointment to his Tonbridge friends. It was no excuse, however, as he concluded with an air of pained affront, for angry letters and unjustifiable charges.

Sadly, however, much more would be said in anger in succeeding days. Thus the Tunbridge Wells Tradesmen's Association's next regular meeting on 2nd September 1884 found Mr. Clifford again in full flood. His town's claims to the long-looked-for Middle school having originated, as he claimed, with the Tradesmen's Association, he felt the gravest concern that things appeared to have come to a standstill. He had looked forward daily to seeing foundations dug on the St.

John's site. Whilst Tunbridge Wells stood still, the opposition were ever more persevering. There appeared to be some malevolent "block or stoppage" on the Skinners' Company's part...

Mr. W.C. Cripps

At this point, the association's harassed secretary was asked to turn up the minutes of past meetings to refresh members' minds. A hurried glance readily yielded facts enough to fuel further debate. The matter had indeed been under consideration for more than nine or ten years. In 1881 too, when the Company appeared to have decided against Tunbridge Wells, the then Association President, Mr. W. C. Cripps' resolution, that the choice of a Tonbridge site was manifestly unjust to Tunbridge Wells, had plainly fired such a broadside as Tunbridge Wells' claims needed at that juncture.

Argument, however, as to the prime movers did little to help in the present. Nor did Mr. Argyle wholly agree that the Tradesmen's Association had initiated Tunbridge Wells action. Had not a certain body of Tunbridge Wells citizens on a certain Monday morning taken possession to a certain extent of Tonbridge Town Hall, and by their vigorous intervention ensured that "that meeting was broken up?" Indeed it had — in February 1875. The Tunbridge Wells Committee had sprung from their own town's meeting hurriedly summoned thereafter to stake its own claim in the face of Tonbridgian assumptions.

Not that Mr. Argyle sought to labour his point. To his credit, as it appears, he took pains to analyse the current impasse in patient, even generous, terms. The Company had, indeed, as he now appreciated, entered into a quiet and for long well-concealed engagement with the inhabitants of Tonbridge. Nor had the Tunbridge Wells spokesmen felt themselves to be making much headway until the full implications of the word "parish" revived their hopes and determination. Meanwhile, as he freely allowed, the Company had very honourably tried to fulfil its pledge to Tonbridge, and from that time had been unwilling partners in the undertaking, which the country's legislature had thought fit to confide to its custody. The Company in the circumstances had felt itself compelled to adopt delaying tactics, its lawyers offering all manner of objections to the vendor's title. In a word, the Skinners were unwilling purchasers, as Mr. Hopwood, the present owner, had remarked to Mr. Argyle, when they had lately met.

Understanding as he might be of the Company's embarrassment, neither Mr. Argyle nor his fellow tradesmen could, however, yield for a moment in their own pressure. Whatever the Company's commitment to Tonbridge, Tunbridge Wells felt sorely let down too. An abandonment of the St. John's site would be a grievous affront to the long list of generous subscribers. Nor did his audience demur when Mr. Argyle suggested in more militant mood that it would further the town's cause, if the Association were once again to represent its opinion, that the present delay was entirely due to inaction, supineness, unwillingness — or whatever term they liked to employ — of the Skinners' Company, and that as Trustees of the charities concerned its members ought to carry out their trust.

To this the meeting duly gave unanimous assent, directing, as so often in matters of this kind, that its judgement be sent not merely to the Skinners' Company and the Charity Commissioners, but also to the Prime Minister, the Leader of the Opposition, the Attorney General, the Privy Council Committee for Education, as also nearer home to the town's school committee and the Local Board. Whatever the reaction of the other recipients, the Local Board readily endorsed the tradesmen's views a few days later, by despatching its own letter to the Company requesting "greater diligence in future to ensure the St. John's site's purchase". Mr. Cheverton's suggestion at the Board's meeting that the town should seek an alternative site was quickly, but firmly, rejected by Mr. Browell.

Meanwhile in its issue reporting the Tradesmen's and the Local Board's deliberations, the local press retailed yet another letter to the Spectator from Mr. Homersham Cox's ever eloquent pen. Mr. Browell was by no means to be allowed the last word. Writing with the Commissioners' first draft scheme of 1875 before him, as he declared, Mr. Cox once more made much of those surplus funds which were then to fund a school "in or near the town of Tonbridge". Furthermore that draft scheme would still have accorded the citizens of Tonbridge valuable privileges, as in particular the right to elect governors. All these privileges his fellow townsmen had relinquished to achieve their prime end. Never a syllable had then been uttered regarding Tunbridge Wells. Since then, despite the Company's repeated protests at the misapplication of its money and the townsmen's vigorous complaint, the Commissioners' breach of faith still stood for all to behold. Tonbridge's recent petition to Parliament, signed as it was by seven hundred residents, including clergymen, magistrates, and all the town's principal inhabitants, fairly expressed the town's righteous indignation. The charges were grave, as Mr. Cox concluded, nor would they be refuted by "big words and blistering assertions". A powerful case, as its spokesman certainly believed, and most forcefully expressed.

It was against the background of this continuing war of words that men in Tunbridge Wells awaited the Company's reply to the Tradesmen's and the Local Board's critical representations with such patience as these increasingly anxious bodies could still muster. Nor were the Company's courteous replies calculated entirely to allay local fears, when in due course they arrived. The Company, Mr. Draper, the Clerk, observed, was not responsible for present delays. He could still not inform the Local Board whether the site's vendors were now in a position to give such title as was necessary. He did, however, expect shortly to see the Company's solicitor — and trusted that early next month some progress would have been made.

Next month, November, nonetheless found Mr. Argyle still steering a delicate course between downright denunciation of the Company and such cautious optimism as could sustain the flow of subscriptions to the Middle School Fund. Not that he could entirely smother his feelings at the Trademen's meeting, when the Skinners' Company's reply was read, disclaiming responsibility but blaming the Commissioners. It was all very well to say that, as he averred, but the Company's refusal to sign the purchase contract, conditional on approval of title, was the only conceivable cause for delay. Even so — with thoughts of those promised subscriptions still unpaid — things were pretty well settled now, and he hoped...

At long, long last too his hopes seemed finally fulfilled. In the issue of 21st November 1884 the Courier's faithful reporter felt it safe to exult and spread the good tidings. Within the past few days, as he delighted to tell, an agreement had been signed by the Skinners' Company and

Messrs. Hopwood, more than one member of the family being, as it transpired, involved. He had it too on good authority that no difficulty would be raised by the Charity Commissioners, and the matter appeared therefore " in a fair way to be finally settled". It had been, as he reflected, nearly a decade since the Honourable F. G. Molyneux chaired the first and crucial Town Hall meeting, which launched the town's campaign. Many active in this most important work had passed away. The long list of subscribers' names appearing in his journal's columns would form a "curious commentary" on the length of time required to bring about any public good. The advantages would be for future generations to enjoy, as the children of those who had so unweariedly carried the matter on year after year had almost passed beyond its benefits. Hearty congratulations, nonetheless, to all concerned.

It is of interest to note some vagueness and discrepancy in the Courier writer's comments in these exciting days. If an agreement had indeed been signed in November 1884, he could still understand — from "reliable sources" — in his 21st January 1885 issue that the contract would be signed within a week! Euphoria none the less reigned supreme, not least in our writer's mind. Whilst the new school's foundation stone would most likely not be laid before Michaelmas 1885, the ceremony would "probably be performed by royalty".

Things had indeed moved forwards, and relatively fast. Before January's end the press could categorically report that the site's purchase money had been lodged in the Skinner's Company's hands, together with £50 to cover the vendors' expenses. A further sum would, however, be required to compensate the site's present tenant and for incidental expenses.

Urgent attention was now accordingly called to the appeal in the advertisement columns, a particular plea being directed to those ladies and gentlemen, who had come to the town since the project was first mooted. To them especially the new school would yield the greatest gain.

We may note at this stage the names of other distinguished residents with generous contributions swelling the growing list, as of John Deacon Esq. £500, J. Stone Wigg Esq. £100, T.Field Gibson £100. Among the local Committee's activists, Mr. Browell proffered his £50, Messrs. Argyle and Clifford their £5 each. The conversion of promises to payment now became of paramount importance.

Nor did it seem even now that the question of title had been irrevocably settled between the Company's solicitors and Messrs. Hopwood, as Mr. Argyle was compelled to admit to Mr Howard at the Local Board's February meeting. He could add, however, his complete confidence that the matter would be settled before the 25th March, the latest date permitted by the Commissioners. To Mr. Briggs' question as to when a foundation stone would be laid, Mr. Browell could only reply that he had nothing further to tell.

In Tonbridge meanwhile, as all Tunbridge Wells will still have uneasily reflected, if a battle had been lost, the war must still go on. Such was certainly the intention of Mr. Homersham Cox and his friends. A determined, concerted effort might yet save the day. Even at this eleventh hour, Tonbridge might yet trump Tunbridge Wells' ace. Another appeal to Parliament might yet redress Tonbridge's wrongs. A carefully prepared campaign could still prevail.

Publicised to the full in mid February 1885, and supported by Mr. Cox's forcefully reasoned letter to the editors not only of the limited local press but to the London daily papers too, a crisply worded memorial to the Charity Commissioners set the scene:

> "Sir, the proceedings of the Skinners' Company with regard to the Skinners' Company's Middle Class School will be brought under the consideration of the House of Commons early in the next session by an MP, who will move for an enquiry upon the subject. Application of funds provided for a school at Tonbridge towards a school at Tunbridge Wells appears to us contrary to the good faith and statutory obligations of the Commissioners. In these circumstances we ask the Commissioners to stay proceedings, until the result of the application to Parliament is ascertained".

Signed, as it was, by the Vicar of Tonbridge, the Headmaster of Tonbridge School, both Tonbridge Churchwardens and the Chairman of the Tonbridge Local Board, this must surely carry substantial weight.

Nor was Mr. Cox's own well publicised letter any less vigorous. The Company's £20,000 offer was only made in view of the general realization that slow accumulation of "surplus funds" would unreasonably delay a new school for Tonbridge. Only after obtaining possession of £20,000, and not before, had the Commissioners disclosed their intention of building the school in Tunbridge Wells. "There is such confidence", he added, "in the impartiality of public partners that the House will be reluctant to condemn the Commissioners without the strongest evidence. That evidence, however, will be produced and one good result will follow from that discussion, namely that benefactors will henceforth be more cautious about parting with the money, where there is any risk of the Charity Commissioners getting hold of it".

It might still have been thought significant that no local Kent MP was named as the gentleman to raise matters in the Commons. It would again be left to the member for Ipswich to fulfill this role. So too the only letter printed in the local journals in comment upon Mr. Cox' charges saw things in a very different light from that rabid partisan. Addressing himself in the first place to the London Daily News — his letter subsequently copied locally — Mr. H. Watts Mason of Primrose Hill, Tonbridge, lent his firm support to the Commissioners' intentions. "Has not the decaying town of Tonbridge a large public-endowed school and much more than its necessity required? Surely Tunbridge Wells with its increasing number of inhabitants and great educational wants has prior claim. The Commissioners would be much to blame, if they started a second endowed school at Tonbridge and continued to compel Tunbridge Wells boys to travel five miles". Not that the men of Tunbridge Wells, the writer suggested, were all that they might be. "Many of them are only too glad to stagnate, as was shown recently in determined efforts to reject a Charter of Incorporation for their town. A good school will have its effect on the rising generation at any rate, and perhaps induce the educationalists of the town to look after the better education of their poorer brethren, who are sadly neglected so far". The soured comment, it may be thought, of someone enamoured of neither his own community, nor of the rival township.

There were others too at this juncture, no doubt, willing to lend Tunbridge Wells support in the final haul. Nor do its residents appear to have been unduly alarmed by the bogey of Commons debate. As March passed through April into May, the Tradesmen's

Association purred with self-satisfaction. With the receipt of the Skinners' Company's solicitor's letter of 25th March, 1885, to Messrs. Stone, Simpson and Sons — read to his fellow members by Mr. Argyle with unrestrained delight — surely no last minute obstacle could now prevent the consummation of their hopes.

> "Dear Sir, in reply to your letter received yesterday, I have investigated the title to the lands agreed to be purchased from Mr. Samuel Weymouth Hopwood and others and have certified to the Commissioners that in my opinion the title shown by the abstracts is good and marketable. The draft conveyance is with the vendors' solicitors for approval, and if they show ordinary diligence, the purchase should be completed immediately after Easter."

One sad note, however, had still to be struck. Mr. Clifford's letter of resignation from the association had also to be reported to the meeting. His mission accomplished, that persistent questioner would be questioning no more.

A few days later the Tonbridge townsmen's petition against the removal of Judd's Free School from Tonbridge to Tunbridge Wells had been duly handed in at the House of Commons by Mr. Collings, the obliging member for Ipswich. Any qualms, however, which might otherwise have been stirred within Tunbridge Wells breasts, were readily allayed by simultaneous receipt of a further letter from Mr. Rhodes, the Company's solicitor. The Commissioners' order confirming the site's sale had at last been received. Might he now, please, be authorized to pay to the vendors' solicitor the £50 which the local committee had undertaken to pay towards the cost of deducing and investigating the land's title?

Matters now moved fast indeed. Saturday, 6th June 1885, found Messrs. Argyle and Browell, together with their solicitor, Mr. Simpson, and Mr. Day, the site's outgoing tenant, happily awaiting Mr. Rhodes' arrival to take possession of the site at 2 p.m. on that day. It is true that Mr. Rhodes' late arrival caused Mr. Browell's departure before the deed was formally done. No serious hitch, however, ensued. Mr. Rhodes arrived in good order, if late, and was duly shown over the site. The tenant received compensation for displacement and formal possession was taken by Mr. George Edwards, who had thoughtfully provided himself with a new padlock, chain and clasp and finally fastened the gate. As the Courier observed, the matter might now ' be regarded as complete". All that remained was for any laggard subscribers to pay up.

Happily, too, any strained relations in the recent past were relieved, as it must have appeared, by the Clerk of the Skinners' Company's generous letter of 12th June to the town's school committee conveying the Company's resolution of the previous day, that cordial thanks be given to the inhabitants of Tunbridge Wells for providing the site's purchase money... and that a copy of the resolution be forwarded to the committee instrumental in raising subscriptions for the purpose. So, too, that committee and its friends must have been especially delighted when Messrs. Hopwood, the site's vendors, proffered their own contribution of £100, as the fund looked to its triumphant close.

The School c. 1900

CHAPTER 5

BUILDING AT LAST

Their petition presented, the Tonbridge inhabitants' grievances would not be further ventilated by Mr. Collings' question in the Commons before August 1885.

At its July meeting in the meantime, the Tunbridge Wells Tradesmen's Association had wound up its own campaign by readily resolving on its President's proposal that "the Association regarded with the utmost satisfaction the completion of the committee's work and respectfully suggested that it was now time for some testimonial to be given to Mr. Argyle for his invaluable service during the ten years the movement was afoot."

In reply, Mr. Argyle once again referred to that now almost legendary occasion when staunch Tunbridge Wells citizens repaired to Tonbridge to break up that town's family gathering in 1875. No word of this conclave had been vouchsafed to Tunbridge Wells. It had been only upon information laid by a certain Mr. Elliott, as we now delight to read, in view of the notice of the meeting seen by him "on one of his piscatorial expeditions to Tonbridge" that those doughty warriors sallied forth. Sadly, as he now observed, most of that gallant band's children were now too old to benefit by their parents' protestations. Their labours would be more for the benefit of prosperity (sic). *(Surely the type setter's lapse, gentle reader, not Mr. Argyle's.)*

Mr. Collings' question was at length asked on 4th August 1885. Were not the Commissioners' actions in gross violation of their statutory powers? Pending an enquiry into the working of the Endowed Schools Act would not the Charity Commissioners postpone expenditure of the endowment in question in order that the grave charges brought by Tonbridge inhabitants might be enquired into?

Mr. Stanhope's reply for the Government of the day can have left the Tonbridge faction in no doubt, that by this stage the game, at least the original game, was up. The Skinners' Company's offer of £20,000, as he insisted, had indeed been made from sources independent of Sir Andrew Judd's foundation and wholly unconnected with Tonbridge for a school "in or near the parish of Tonbridge". The school's position had been left open at the express desire of the Skinners' Company, as we recall the Commissioners earlier maintaining. A Middle School Scheme in the form agreed by the Company having been duly approved by Her Majesty, the Commissioners then having very properly received representations from both towns, the Commissioners had elected to place the school at Tunbridge Wells. Approval of site had been expressly reserved to the Commissioners. They had acted upon the wide considerations of the respective localities. Their decision could not be reversed.

No one could have expected the men of Tonbridge to receive this weighty judgment without a whimper. Nor did they. Repeated questioning of Mr. Stanhope by Mr. R. K. Causton, himself a Skinner, we recall, elicited no more favourable reply. The Tonbridge Free Press likewise fumed in vain. No man of Tonbridge, it raged, could accept that "in or near the parish of Tonbridge" had been introduced at the Skinners' Company's desire. Nor was it true that both towns offered sites simultaneously, as Mr. Stanhope had stated Tunbridge Wells had both needed, and been given, more time to come forward with a site. Prejudice had persistently prevailed. The Chief Commissioner himself had settled on Tunbridge Wells at the outset.

Nor were Mr. Homersham Cox's efforts to widen the issue by further vigorous correspondence in the national press of greater avail.

In vain did he insist that the Commissioners' conduct was of no mere local interest, but involved the gravest question as to the management of charitable trusts throughout the land.
In vain did he stress the irreconcilable nature of Mr. Stanhope's statements with the Skinners' Company's own declarations.

The new school would certainly be sited on the St John's site in Tunbridge Wells.
And yet... if only the pressure could still be maintained upon both Commissioners and Company, might not the aggrieved sons of Tonbridge still hope to salvage something of their hopes?

In Tunbridge Wells hopes, of course, continued conspicuously high. Subscriptions flowed steadily in. The Final and Complete List of Subscribers totalled some £2,500 — if every promise were in fact fulfilled. Among names destined to remain for years among the town's

E. Waymark, Esq.

Mr. E. H. Burnell

prominent traders we may note those of R. W. Weekes Esq. (£20) and E. Waymark Esq. (5 guineas). A contribution of 2 guineas came in these last days too from the Courier Printing Press — a timely and grateful gesture in respect of an undertaking, whose varying fortunes had yielded copy and comment to its presses for so long.

In Tunbridge Wells, indeed the year 1885 had ended well. As the New Year drew in however, doubt and dismay yet again threatened to raise their familiar heads. Surely by now some activity should be evident upon the site. Times were hard this winter, even in the more fashionable spa, and the labouring classes hoped week by week for the chance of employment in digging foundations and preparation of the site. No word, however, came as yet of building as yet of building.

The members of the Skinner's Company nominated to serve as the new school's govenors had indeed six months ago, on 30th June 1885, recommended that the Company's Surveyor be instructed to submit plans and estimates forthwith. This recommendation being approved by the full Court of the Company ten days later, the Surveyor was formally required to submit his proposals within no more than two weeks. "Proper school buildings" were to be provided for 200 boys with all necessary "fittings". A Headmaster's house should be included also, if no suitable residence could be obtained in the neighbourhood. Drains and fences being allowed for too, the total estimate, including architect's charges, should not exceed £10,000, or £8,000, if a headmaster's house could be obtained elsewhere. Expenditure of more than £40 per boy, exclusive of the Headmaster's house, would, as the governors ruled be 'an excessive outlay". Nor were the Surveyor, Mr. E. H. Burnell's, proposals, duly presented on 23rd July 1885, found acceptable in their original form. Not until 13th October did the governors feel able to recommend that the Surveyor's revised plans be finalized and specifications prepard with a view to the Commissioner's consent under Clause 9 of the School Scheme.

A total of £6,675, it was now estimated, should suffice for the Main Building. Drainage and Water Supply would call for £125, Walling (£200), Gates (£100) and Fence (£200) should be obtainable for a total of £500. With Levelling and Planting calling for a further £200, the grand estimated total reached £7,500, increased by a 10% addition for Architect's commission and Contingencies, to a final figure of £8,250. A month later the Court of the Company ordered submission of the plans to the Charity Commissioners.

It had all, however, taken time, and when at the Tunbridge Wells Local Board's meeting in January 1886 Mr. Hatch bluntly enquired of Mr. Argyle, what was the exact position of his committee's negotiations with the Skinners Company, and when were the buildings likely to begin, Mr. Argyle could only answer that he was as anxious as everybody else. He could reveal indeed that the Company had considered its Surveyors first plans too expensive and that revised proposals had been called for. He too, however, was concerned that at a time of grievous unemployment, the Company failed to avail itself of an opportunity to provide employment in at least leveling the site. Within the same month, the Tradesmen's annual report similarly deplored this failure to provide employment, whilst reiterating its belief that Mr. Argyle's services should be recognized "in some substantial manner".

The Commissioners' wheels, however, in the meantime had turned slowly, if more rapidly, it might be thought, than at other times in this long- drawn tale. In reporting submission of the Company's plans to Mr. Joseph Clark, the Commissioner's own architect, the Commission in early February moved also to ensure the infant school's endowment, by requesting transfer of sums held for this purpose to the Official Trustee in trust for the Foundation. Nor did Mr. Clark's examination of the plans delay building unreasonably. Before the end of February, they were back with the governors with Mr. Clark's blessing, subject only to minor modifications, bringing also the Commissioners' authority to seek tenders for the fulfilment of the work. The minor modifications required would involve additional cost, as the Surveyor judged, of "quite £200". The governors nonetheless happily agreed that tenders be now invited.

These came in also with remarkable speed. Nor did the Company delay its decision. Choosing the lowest of ten prices submitted, the governors awarded the contract to Messrs.Oakley and Drake, the figure approved being no more than £5,300. Messrs. Hall, Bedall and Co. of London had named £5,400 as their figure. Messrs. Punnett of

Tonbridge and other aspirants drawn from London, Dover, Maidstone and Margate in each case asked for more.

Whether, *or not*, the interested parties within Tunbridge Wells were privy to the Company's own estimate of the building's likely cost, they were certainly made aware of the far lower tenders submitted.

Mr. W. Oakley   Mr. A. Drake

Yet again a sense of disappointment and frustration gripped many townsmen's minds.

The local press commentator could only express his belief that the building proposed was but the preliminary to a further enlargement. It might be thought too, he suggested, as of a temporary nature — awaiting the assurance of a successful launch, before enhancement and the crowning glory of a house for its Headmaster.

Be that as it may, the legal formalities ensued, Messrs. Oakley and Drake duly contracted to fulfill the governors' requirements, subject to a bond in the sum of £1,000 and two "sufficient sureties". The local press readers would indeed have been delighted to read on 21st May 1886 not only that the building contract had been signed, but that work had already begun, the site had been grubbed out, and the ground already being cleared for foundations.

Nor could the contractors be in any way faulted in respect of speed and diligence, when once the work began. Mr. Alfred Drake's withdrawal from the Oakley and Drake's partnership in July in no way hindered proceedings. Another withdrawal, however, can only have been received by his fellow members with the deepest regret and renewed appreciation of his years of yeoman toil. Mr. Argyle himself had felt it necessary at the Local Board's June meeting to submit his letter of resignation from that body on grounds of ill health — conceivably exacerbated by his dogged endeavours. As he begins to withdraw from our stage, we may note with pleasure the generosity with which his resignation letter proceeds also to acknowledge the liberality of the Company, in giving up a portion of the school site to widen the road and permit a 9 foot path in front of the school.

He had begun by now to tidy his final statement of the town's subscription fund, even as, within Skinners' Hall, the Clerk and Surveyor applied their minds to the stone laying ceremony planned for October. The governors furthermore authorized release of stock to the tune of £6,000 to ensure the contractors' payment and to contend, if need be, with any emergency arising in the intervening weeks. There were Tithe Rent charges upon the site, for instance, which needed to be redeemed. A redemption payment of £32.5s.4d. was duly approved in lieu of payments, to the impressively titled Impropriator, of £1 per annum, and to the Vicar, presumably of Tonbridge, of a modest five shillings.

Friday, 13th August, found Mr. Argyle able and happy to present his final statement. Falling a little short of earlier anticipation, subscriptions received had totalled £2,356.10s.6d., to which was to be added interest payments of £16.6s.8d on money deposited at Messrs. Molyneux and Co's Bank. After payment of purchase price to Messrs. Hopwood, advertising, printing and law costs throughout the eleven years' campaign and the sum of £30 as compensation for Mr. Day, the site's previous tenant, a balance remained in hand of £40.16s.6d.

As the fund's secretary from its inception, Mr. Argyle deserved indeed the unstinted gratitude and congratulations of his fellow citizens, as they combined to plan their testimonial in recognition of his inestimable service to their town. Further to his energetic effort on the new school's behalf he had lately, we learn, been the secretary also of an emergency fund for the relief of unemployment in the town. This fund also had raised around £2,400 in the course of a very few weeks. He would be longest remembered however, for his sustained determination to win his town its school.

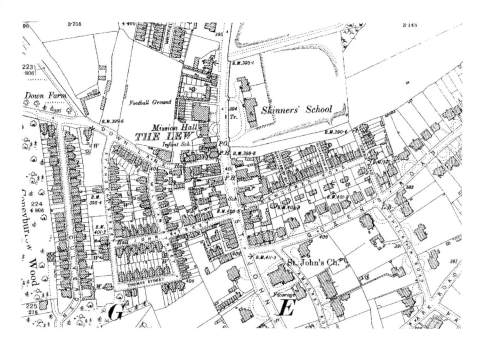

Ordnance Survey map of St. John's area, 1897

Well might Mr. Hatch describe him, as the final figures were revealed as "the most independent man Tunbridge Wells had brought forth", whilst Mr. Clements could speak of a fearlessness and independence which were "refreshing charactistics in Tunbridge Wells".

As the new school rose rapidly and without sign now of further problem, preparations for the stone-laying ceremony likewise proceeded smoothly. The Master, Mr. Lewis Boyd Sebastian, the Wardens and other members of the Company would entrain from Cannon Street Station, adjacent to their hall, on 27th October 1886 at 10.25 a.m. The ceremony would take place at noon precisely. An invitation by Mr. Samuel Wix, a Past Master of the Company, to luncheon at his Broadwater Down house was gratefully accepted. The Vicar of the parish, that is the relatively new parish of St. John's, Tunbridge Wells, in which the new school stood, should be invited to be present. The Surveyor too was authorised to purchase the "necessary tools" for the proper laying of the stone at a cost not exceeding £10. The scene was efficiently set, if without much opportunity or encouragement for townspeople to associate themselves with the occasion, or pay their respects to the founding fathers.

64

Little, if any, advance notice of the stone-laying had been given to the town at large. Not until five days before the event could the local press inform its readers of its "understanding" that the foundation stone would be laid on Wednesday next. The building having grown so rapidly, he might well add that he found it "somewhat singular" that the ceremony took place now, for Mr. Oakley had pushed on so rapidly, that the building was now "almost two thirds completed". Nor in reporting of the occasion one week later, could our scribe conceal his regret that this long awaited moment became something "of a private character in connection with the Skinners' Company", and that the town had been deprived of the pomp and circumstance, which it felt the occasion demanded.

At the end of the day, however, none could deny that the stone had been well and truly laid — beside the North Wing's entrance portals, overlooking, as it still does, all who entered the fledgling school. However small the local attendance, it had been laid with such good measure of propriety and respect, as had always been due to the Company's public occasions.

Conveyed from the station in some six carriages supplied by Mr. Waghorn of Mount Ephraim, the governors and their attendant officers had been first received by Mr. Oakley. Having fulfilled a preliminary tour of the rapidly rising buildings, they had expressed themselves well pleased, as it was reported, with the masonry in particular adorning the exterior walls. A square platform having been erected beside the entrance doorway — the whole covered by a tarpaulin awning and railed off with red baize — the assembled company had then cautiously climbed the broad flight of steps to assume their appointed places. Groups of flowers, "kindly lent by Mrs. Allnut of Culverden Park" lent distinction to the boarding.

A convenient aperture having been left in the wall for its insertion, the foundation stone, a fine piece of Wiltshire Sandstone inscribed with the facts and names of the occasion, patiently awaited the Master's hand. The Company's armorial bearings, sadly, as yet were only sketched in. Time had not permitted the final touch. Beneath the stone's resting place lay a further circular aperture awaiting the insertion of a jar containing documents relating to the school and its foundation, a number of coins, bronze, silver and gold and fresh from the mint, and a copy of an issue of a London daily paper. These having been duly deposited and the aperture cemented — a treasure unsuspected by generations of boys and masters passing beneath in years ahead — the stone was slowly lowered into place. With the aid of a handsome chased silver trowel, its ivory handle delicately designed and polished, as our observant reporter relates, and appropriate taps with the accompanying mallet, the Master formally assured its appropriate location. It remained only for the Clerk of the Works, Mr. Fagg, Junior, on his spirit level's evidence to declare it well and truly laid.

His task fulfilled, the Master proceeded to address the small gathering as to the significance of the occasion and the negotiations which had preceded it. It may be doubted, however, whether his references to the needs of Tonbridge School for a new scheme involving higher fees to be paid by parents able and willing to afford them, meant much to the few Tunbridge Wells ears present. For Tunbridge Wells, the past was the past. It quietly rejoiced in its new acquisition and happily murmured its gratitude to its generous benefactors. Nor were the workmen engaged on the site any less delighted, when they too were assembled to hear the Master present Mr. Oakley with £10 to distribute among them, as he thought best.

Mr.J.F.Wadmore of Tonbridge and the Architect, Mr. E.H. Burnell, had also spoken, the former as the senior Skinner present to invite the Master to perform his allotted role, the latter to stress the prime advantage of the present building, that it was capable of enlargement - almost, as he expressed it, to any extent.

At this point Mr. G. Glanville presented himself with the intention of taking a photograph, the platform party arranging themselves on either side of the stone. The Master, his silver trowel in hand, properly held the position of honour. Unfortunately by this time the weather was unfavourable for photography, a misty rain had fallen in the latter part of the proceedings. To achieve his end, Mr. Glanville accordingly found it desirable to require further planks projecting from the platform, thence to direct his lens, as our observer expressed it from a "somewhat hazardous position". Happily the result of this intrepid manoeuvre may still be appreciated today (*see opposite*).

No recording, however, survives of a further incident noted as an unofficial part of the programme. A professional military band, as it was described, previously performing in a neighbouring road, promptly struck up the National Anthem, as proceedings appeared to be drawing to their close. Nor was further time lost before the company was driven off to lunch with Mr. Wix in Broadwater Down. The first Skinners' Day, as the local press ventured to name it, had ended.

Laying of the Foundation Stone, 27th.October 1886

In almost all respects, it had been a much quieter and more limited occasion than might have been expected. If the Tonbridge Free Press were to be believed, "only three or four persons were present besides those directly concerned". This may well have been the jaundiced viewpoint of a disappointed suitor and not fully in keeping with the facts. It nonetheless stung those Tunbridge Wells stalwarts, who had fought so doggedly and long. Still vitally interested and able to put pen to paper, Mr. Argyle felt constrained to write to his own town's editor in pained rejoinder. That the Tonbridge scribe's inability to rise superior to his feelings of resentment should have led him to minimise the importance of "one of the noblest and most beneficent institutions ever established in Tunbridge Wells" filled him, as was only to be expected, with the utmost indignation. Reference to the paucity of attendance at the stone-laying he felt particularly unkind and wholly uncalled for. All had proceeded at the Company's wish, its customary routine had been observed in all things. Bands, banners and a grand procession could otherwise have readily been mounted. It was in every way unfair and ungenerous to suggest that Tunbridge Wells took no interest in its new school.

Not that Tunbridge Wells feathers remained ruffled for long. Building proceeded speedily as ever. Optimists indeed looked to the school's opening at Easter 1887. The Governors meanwhile required their Clerk to prepare an advertisement for its first Headmaster. The Surveyor too was instructed to prepare rough plans for a Headmaster's house to cost, inclusive of fittings and all contingent charges, not more than £2,000. The Clerk's draft readily approved, subject only to the requirement that the age of candidates be not more than 40, the advertisement had appeared in no fewer than thirteen national or local newspapers and periodicals before 1886 was ended.

The Times, Daily News, Daily Telegraph, Standard, Daily Chronicle, Leeds Mercury, Liverpool Mercury, Manchester Guardian, Kent and Sussex Courier, Tunbridge Wells Advertiser, Tonbridge Free Press, Spectator and Saturday Review were all engaged in the urgent task of the initial appointment. A note forwarded to all candidates that no list of governors could be made available to them, "as the Governors do not wish to be personally canvassed, at any rate not until a first selection shall have been made", may perhaps be fairly taken as a sidelight on a common Victorian practice.

In the event, 79 candidates made application for the one vacant post. Interview of eight selected candidates on 1st February 1887 led to a second interview of five gentlemen by the Company's full Court on 17th February, when the choice fell upon the Rev. Frederick G. Knott, MA. of Magdalene College, Cambridge, an Assistant Master at Dulwich College. He would remain at his post for thirty seven years, a legend in his lifetime.

Rev. Frederick G. Knott, MA (Cantab)

CHAPTER 6

OPENED FOR BUSINESS

There had been hopes, as has been mentioned, that the new school might open its doors after Easter 1887. Much, however, still remained to be done. Tuition fees required to be settled, a prospectus prepared, assistant staff appointed. Much discussion must ensue between the Company's Clerk, Mr. Draper, and the Headmaster-designate before local advertisement could invite registration of the school's first entry. The school could plainly not be ready for its first pupils before the autumn.

Meanwhile the town's tradesmen and others held lively discussion as to how the town might best mark the inception of an institution for which it had worked so long.

Might not the funding of a Jubilee Scholarship or Exhibition, in the Good Queen's Golden Jubilee Year, be an appropriate buttress to the new foundation?

Should not the town also mount a public reception for the Worshipful Company, whose members, it was confidently presumed, would wish to inaugurate their handsome foundation in an appropriately public fashion?

Would it not be a kindly gesture for the Tradesmen's Association to vary the date of its annual dinner and to invite members of the Skinners' Company to share its festive board on a day nearer the date of the school's inception?

As in the previous October, however, the Company courteously declined the prospect of pomp or ceremony on or around the school's first day.

Mr. Knott pressed steadily ahead with his plans, seeking and obtaining authority to appoint a Chief Assistant, a Modern Language Master and a Junior Assistant, at annual salaries of £200, £150 and £100 respectively. The average number of boys to each master, the governors ruled should be 25. The governors' subsequent vote of £150 for the year 1887, for the single term concerned presumably, "for maintaining assistant masters, as also a proper school plant and apparatus and otherwise furthering the current objects of the school" must surely imply that the full complement of masters would not be immediately appointed. Meanwhile we may note an unexpectedly early use of the word "plant" in a school connection. A further resolution accorded the Headmaster £1 weekly for the hiring of a caretaker. The Headmaster's own salary would be £100 per annum, plus an agreed capitation fee of £3 for each boy in attendance, this latter figure to be reviewed, when the school roll exceeded 100. Tuition fees should be £3.10s. per term, the school's scheme requiring that they be not less than £8, nor more than £12 per annum.

All fell into its place in time and Mr. Knott himself was emboldened to express his own hope that the Court of the Skinners' Company would attend the school's opening. Such public inauguration, however, was not to be, as much to the town's disappointment as to Mr. Knott's. The school should first find its feet. Uncertainty too prevailed in respect of likely school numbers. Nor was the bitterness engendered by the long drawn battle lightly to be set aside. Slowly the town accepted that the school's imposing opening was not to be among the high points of its Jubilee Year. The suggestion of a Jubilee Scholarship faded quietly away. The Tradesmen's Association's annual dinner would observe its customary November date. The school would slip quietly into life on Wednesday, 14th September, 1887.

It must be said at once that neither the Headmaster nor his first assistant masters, Mr. P. Shaw Jeffrey, B.A. (Queen's College, Oxford) and Mr. H. E. Pochin, B.A. (King's College, Cambridge) could complain of the extent of local press coverage of the school's first days. They must, however, have remarked an equivocal note in much that they read. Both in the weeks before and after the opening day, fulsome eulogy of the school's building and equipment was all too plainly matched by scarcely veiled criticism of the whole. The town had plainly hoped for more. Initial numbers too were less than those who had worked so hard to win the school, had predicted. The apparent reluctance of the school's governors to join with the town's worthies in festive celebration could only foster misgiving as to the nurture the school might require in its formative years.

We may still read indeed with delight the glowing and most detailed account of the school buildings. We may readily check for ourselves its construction of "red brick from High Brooms Brick Works, relieved by strings and dressings of local sandstone, the external walls flanked by substantial buttresses, with stone weatherings capped by substantial terminals".

We may equally appreciate its roof "covered with Brosley tiles in two tints, suitably interspersed, the top being crowned with a crested ridge". In similarly detailed vein we may delight in its bell turret housing "a nicely toned bell", or in the Schoolroom, "a fine, commodious apartment, lofty, well lighted and in every way adapted to its purpose". We may respond to unstinted praise of "Lord's patent wood block covering, which by deadening the sound of the footfall, does much to ensure the quietness which the work of a schoolroom demands."

We may consider too the present day Librarian's Office, situated at the end of the balcony landing, in its original role as a "comfortable, though rather small sitting room for the Headmaster, containing its fire-place and lighted by an angular oriel window and a second window at the side". We shall certainly be reassured by observation that "an exploration of the basement discloses the fact that efficient provision has been made for all the sanitary requirements of a public school". Games players too may be pleased to read of the extensive ground at the rear of the school which "will afford ample space for outdoor recreation". Their pleasure may, however, be tempered as they read on to learn that "from its present appearance, however, it will probably require a good deal of laying out before such a game as cricket, which is now so popular a feature of a public school curriculum, can be indulged in".

Whatever remained to do in respect of the surrounding ground, the school's buildings had been essentially completed some months before it admitted its first scholars. The only untoward circumstance had been the untimely death of the original Clerk of Works, Mr. Cooper J. Fagg. A blow from a plank falling upon him, as workmen sought to lift it, had so far aggravated his constitutional lung weakness, as we read, as to lead to his death within a few days. His father, Mr. Cooper Fagg Senior, fulfilled his duties until the contract was completed.

At length on the appointed day, Wednesday, 14th September, the school's first intake presented itself at the front of the school. If not unheralded, certainly at this point unsung, the new foundation made its unobtrusive entrance upon the town's scene. The entrance door quietly opened, that door "of solid oak with foliated hinges, label mouldings and carved bosses". Why does the eye today fail to perceive such evident adornments?

Wearing his collegiate cap, hood and gown, as we are told, Mr. Knott opened the school without further ado, by what would become, as he indicated, the school's ordinary routine, merely addressing a few remarks to his assembled charges as to his general intentions regarding their tuition and welfare. Urging his young hopefuls, if he be reported verbatim, to "use their best endeavours to be a credit to their school, he may well have sown the first seeds of the Leopards' Song soon to emerge from his colleague, Mr. Shaw Jeffrey's, fertile mind.

Be that, however, as it may, The Skinners' Middle School was now in being. Fifty-two young townsmen were launched on that first day upon their 9 a.m. to 12.30 p.m., 2 p.m. to 4 p.m. six day treadmill, with half holidays, albeit on Wednesdays and Saturdays — but with evening preparation, need it be said?, to ensure that little time be wasted. A trickle of further entrants raised numbers to 64 by mid October. Local opinion had indeed looked for more, even as many had hoped for more impressive buildings. The beginning had nonetheless been made. That beginning too was in Tunbridge Wells and not in the older town of Tonbridge. Tunbridge Wells most surely had cause to rejoice and be glad, whatever reservations might have been felt that its new school had come to birth, with no sound of trumpets and no beat of drum.

Nor — a happy postscript to the Tunbridge Wells tale — did Tonbridge persistence long go unrewarded. Sir Andrew Judd's Commercial School, the Judd School of today, was in being — in a hired house — no more than one year later. The tale of its birth, however, is for another's pen to tell. Suffice that at long, long last, pressures upon the Skinners' Company to found a Commercial School from surplus Judd Foundation funds bore fruit. The Tonbridge tradesman need no longer feel himself robbed of Sir Andrew's bounty. Honour might be thought to be satisfied in all quarters. The war was over, and both sides might be thought to have won.

CHAPTER 7

Today

The story of the Skinners' School's origins may well be termed a period piece, a cameo of Victorian privilege, pride and persistence. Local rivalries today are rarely so bitterly maintained, or paraded.

Today, where an honourable city company sought to build a single school, stand two proud and fully-fledged schools of distinguished past achievement and a confidence too in their future - Skinner's and Judd. Good friends moreover on every plane, each happily sheltered beneath the Skinners' Company's kindly wing. So too the Company's members of today, the writer confidently believes, will be neither dismayed nor embarrassed by this story of public controversy in a more leisurely age.

Time heals all wounds, and after a hundred years it may safely be told. Nor would the good Sir Andrew, we may feel, have disapproved of the issue of the long running dispute. Boys in both Tonbridge and the adjacent country might now look to benefit from his pious and benevolent intentions.

No longer need any part of the locality harbour its reproach of an earlier school and its governors, that they failed to meet the needs of local boys. The two new schools would happily serve as the keepers of Tonbridge School's conscience, as an understanding Skinner suggested, in the challenging years ahead.

Arms of Sir Andrew Judd

Main Entrance to the School, showing the Foundation Stone
between the windows to the left of the doorway

PART II – THE BUILDINGS

CHAPTER 8

THE ORIGINAL SCHOOL

The original school building of 1886/7, which has been briefly described in Chapter 6 and which is now known as the Main School, is cruciform in plan. The east-west "transept" comprises a West Tower, and an East Tower, linked together on two main levels.

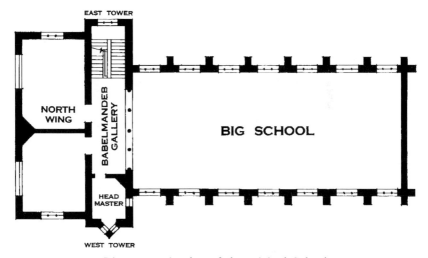

Diagrammatic plan of the original School

In the base of the West Tower is the main entrance, above which is a room that was originally for the Headmaster. This is lighted by an angular oriel window facing west, and a side window facing south.

The East Tower contains a staircase and is linked to the West Tower at Ground floor level by the Entrance Hall. Above this, at first floor level, the Babelmandeb Gallery links the two towers.

The Bab el Mandeb Strait, which features in the School Song of 1894, is a twenty-mile-long strategic shipping lane, linking the Red Sea with the Gulf of Aden and the Indian Ocean. Bab el Mandeb has been variously translated as the Gate of Wailing or Distress, probably because of the number of ships lost trying to get through the Strait in adverse weather.

Babelmandeb Gallery

It was in the strategic Babelmandeb link at The Skinners School that, in former times, those having occasion to see the Headmaster awaited their fate.

To the south of the east-west transept is the original school room or "Big School", now the School Hall. This is some 70 feet long and 30 feet wide, with a lofty arch-braced timber roof supported on stone corbels. On the north wall are four pointed arched openings affording views down to the Big School from the Babelmandeb Gallery. The arches rest on columns of red Mansfield stone with moulded bases and foliated capitals.

On the north side of the transept, the North Wing has been raised, although in a sympathetic manner. It formerly provided class rooms, a porter's box and cloak rooms but it now accommodates the Staff Room

76

The architectural style of the Original School Building is a form of Early English Gothic, the flat stone heads of the principal three-light windows having circular piercings to provide plate tracery.

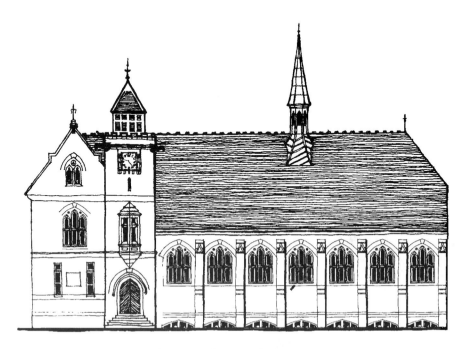

West elevation of Original School Building

The west elevation of the Big School is divided into seven bays by deep buttresses. The elegant flèche surmounting the Big School has diagonally ribbed leadwork aprons rising from the steeply-pitched tiled roof, an octagonal lantern with cusped arched openings, and a slender lead-covered spirelet. The West Tower has three stages, the lowest of which contains the entrance doorway, approached by a square flight of stone steps. The timber doors have ornamental scroll-work hinges, and the stonework surround has a dripstone with foliated terminals. In the central stage is the oriel window, which incorporates a panel with a monogram and the date 1886.

A square clock is set in the top stage of the tower, flanked by colonettes and supported on brackets. The top of the tower is battlemented and has medieval gargoyles at its corners. The tower is surmounted by a raised pyramidal roof and a weather vane.

The North Wing to the left of the West Tower contains the Foundation Stone, mentioned in Chapter 5, giving the date 1886, together with the name of the architect, Edward Henry Burnell and the builder. William Oakley. Well known as a Tunbridge Wells builder, William Oakley was at one time in partnership with the noteworthy Builder/ Developer of parts of the Calverley Estate, William Willicombe.

The West Tower

The East Tower, containing the original staircase, has a gabled top and an extra stage at the base because of the drop in level across the site. The change in level also enabled a crypt-like playground cloister to be provided beneath the Big School. This was originally open on its east side, but the area is now enclosed.

Base of East Tower

On the South Wall of the East Tower is a stone drinking fountain, the spout being in the form of a leopard's head - a motif found in the armorial bearings of the Skinners' Company.

The Leopard Drinking Fountain

CHAPTER 9

THE HEADMASTER'S HOUSE
AND THE SCIENCE SCHOOL

The Architect of the Original School, Edward Henry Burnell, FRIBA, (1819-1892) was appointed Surveyor to the Worshipful Company of Skinners in 1861, a post that he held for some thirty years until his retirement on the grounds of failing health in 1891. In that same year he was offered, and accepted, a seat at the Court as an Honorary Member.(1). E.H. Burnell was articled to the Essex Architect and Surveyor James Beadel, and for a few years afterwards he was with the distinguished architect Sir William Tite, sometime President of the RIBA and of the Cambridge Camden Society. Based in an office at No.32 Bedford Row, London, Burnell was responsible for a good deal of work at Tonbridge School in the 1860s and he was elected a Fellow of the RIBA in 1877.(2). He was proposed by Charles Barry, John Whichcord and Henry Curry.

Burnell's instructions concerning the school at Tunbridge Wells came in 1885 and were to prepare plans for the erection of a Middle School for Boys. This was to be at a cost of £10,000 if a Headmaster's House was to be included, or £8,000 if a suitable residence for the Headmaster could be obtained elsewhere.(3).

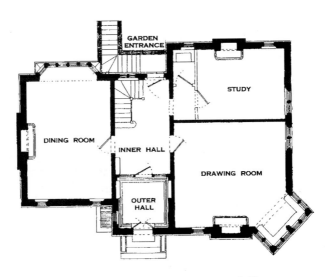

Headmaster's House - Ground Floor

Work on the Original School Building proceeded without a house for the Headmaster at first, and it was in November 1886 that the Court instructed Burnell to prepare rough plans for the Headmaster's House. (4) Further instructions were given in 1889 for tenders to be obtained for the erection of the Headmaster's House, now known as School House, and the quotation from the firm W.J. Mitchell and Co. of Dulwich was accepted in the sum of £2,565. (5).

The original Dining Room, now the Headmaster's Study, and the original Drawing Room, now the School Office, have coved cornices incorporating the armorial bearings of the Skinners Company. Beneath the original Dining Room was the Kitchen, which also served a Boy's Dining Room underneath the original Drawing Room and Study.

Externally, the Headmaster's House is a striking building, with a canted bay window to the former Drawing Room on its south-west corner. Like the Original School Building, the Headmaster's House is faced in red brick with stone dressings and, stylistically, it continues the Gothic tradition. Yet, with features such as the prominent chimney stacks and the hipped dormer, there is something of the Aesthetic Movement about the building too.

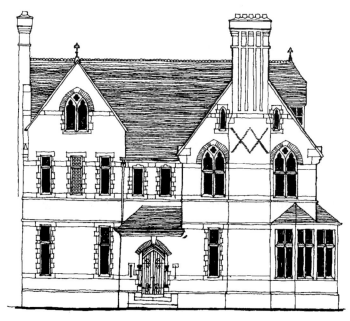

Headmaster's House

At the Foundation Stone laying in October 1886, Burnell recognised that considerably more accommodation would eventually be needed to meet the needs of the town of Tunbridge Wells, but he expressed himself pleased to provide reassurance "that the building was capable of any amount of extension". (6). Positive movement towards extension came in February 1897 with a letter from the Headmaster, the Revd. F.G.Knott, concerning the advisability of an organised Science School. (7).

By that time, the Surveyorship of the Skinners' Company had passed from Burnell to his pupil William Cambell-Jones. Thus it was to Campbell-Jones that instructions came in 1899 to prepare plans for the erection of a proposed workshop and new rooms for the teaching of science at a cost estimated to be £3,000. (8). Rather as Burnell's plans had been subject to the scrutiny of the Commissioners' Architect Joseph Clarke, so Campbell-Jones' plans were duly examined by W.D. Caroe. Tenders were then invited and an order for the additional building was placed with Messrs. Davis and Leaney. (9).

Campbell-Jones' extension southwards from the Big School is sympathetic to his master's work, while moving on from the Gothic tradition and embracing the Aesthetic and Arts and Crafts movements more wholeheartedly. The gabled treatment of the Southern extension has rough-cast in its apex, with tile-hanging below and red brickwork with stone banding.

William Campbell-Jones, FRIBA, (1862-1951) was appointed Surveyor to the Skinners' Company in 1891 and he held the post for some 50 years until 1941. Educated at Haileybury, the Architectural Association, University College London, and the Academy Schools, Campbell-Jones was articled to E.H. Burnell and set up in practice in London in 1887. (10). Like Burnell, Campbell-Jones was also responsible for work at Tonbridge School, a scheme for which he exhibited at the Royal Academy in 1894. Also, he designed the Judd School in Tonbridge.

West Elevation of the Science School

CHAPTER 10

LATER ADDITIONS

While the southern extension to the Big School was being considered, another initiative was taking shape close by. The Vicar of St.John's Church, the Revd. H.E. Eardley had approached the Tunbridge Wells Architects H.H. and E. Cronk to design a Parish Room now known as the Byng Hall, hard up against the southern boundary of The Skinners' School.

The Byng Hall

A letter from the Architects explaining the proposal was sent to the Skinners' Company in February 1899, and was followed by a visit from Alderman H.H. Cronk to Skinners' Hall in London later in that year, permission having been given for windows to over look the school. (11).

Thus, from the outset, the Skinners' School and the Byng Hall impacted upon one another.

Architecturally too, they were cognate, the Byng Hall being again in red brick with stone dressings in a Gothic style and with a steeply sloping pitched roof covered in red tiles.

It was particularly appropriate, therefore, that in 2003 the Byng Hall should become part of the Skinners' School looking, as it does, as though that has always been the case.

Henry Hickman Cronk, a local public figure who preceded Sir David Salomons as Mayor of Tunbridge Wells, was no stranger to the Gothic style of architecture. His contributions to the Tunbridge Wells scene in the 1870s had included St.Peter's Church in Bayhall Road and Beechings Bank, now Lloyds Bank, in Mount Pleasant. The Byng Hall was opened on 17th October 1900 by Admiral Charles Lucas, VC, a relative of the Byng family of Great Culverden that had contributed towards the cost of the project. (12).

The front elevation to St.John's Road has a projecting staircase bay on the left-hand side and a three-light traceried window above the entrance door. Internally, the Hall, now a Theatre, has a balcony at one end. At the back of the Byng Hall, fronting on to Shaftesbury Road, is the former Institute Building, which now accommodates a Music Room on the first floor.

The former St. John's Institute building from Shaftesbury Road

The First World War took a terrible toll of human life, and the names of Masters and former pupils who fell are inscribed in a Memorial on the wall of the Big School near the organ.

This Memorial was designed by the Tunbridge Wells Architect C.H. Strange, and dedicated by the Bishop of Truro in 1920.(14) The memorial is of oak and is Gothic in style, having five panels with cusped heads, divided by clustered columns with moulded caps and bases. Further panelling has since been added, listing the names of the fallen in the Second World War.

Like H.H. Cronk, Charles Hilbert Strange, FRIBA, Architect and Councillor, was another prominent local figure, and is noted for his designs for the Homeopathic Hospital and the pavilion at the Nevill Cricket Ground in Tunbridge Wells. C.H. Strange also produced a design for a memorial sports pavilion, which is preserved at the Reference Library in Tunbridge Wells. In the event, however, the memorial pavilion, which is close to Currie Road, was designed by another local Architect, Stanley Philpot, an old boy of the school. (14).

For the record, the more recent additions at the rear of the School include the 1958/60 "New Wing" by R.N. Wakelin, FRIBA; the Knox Wing of 1979/80; the Cecil Beeby Building, which was opened by his widow Mrs Muriel Beeby in September 2002; and the Leopard Building of 1993/4 by Malcolm Hollis Associates. However, the landmark buildings on the main St.John's Road frontage remain the Original School Building and the Headmaster's House, together with their slightly newer neighbour, the Byng Hall.

Stanley Philpot's design for the Pavilion

Pupils were first admitted into the Original School in 1887 and, in that same year the foundation stone of another great Gothic building of High Brooms red brick was being laid in another part of the town, namely at the Tractarian Church of St.Barnabas in Stanley Road.

Together, that church and Burnell's buildings at the Skinners' School form the prime examples in Tunbridge Wells of what might be termed 'the Keble College, Oxford genre'. It was a style of architecture that was much derided in Oxford in the 1920s, but which is now praised and admired. Similarly, in Tunbridge Wells, the historian Richard Cobb once dismissed the Skinners' School as "borstal-like buildings in livid brick" but, again, taste has moved on towards full circle.

Today, Tunbridge Wells can be grateful to the ancient Skinners' Company, to its 16th century benefactors Thomas Hunt and Lawrence Atwell, and to its Surveyor E.H. Burnell for a school that is not only a respected place of learning for all classes of society, but an ornament to one of the principal approach roads to the town.

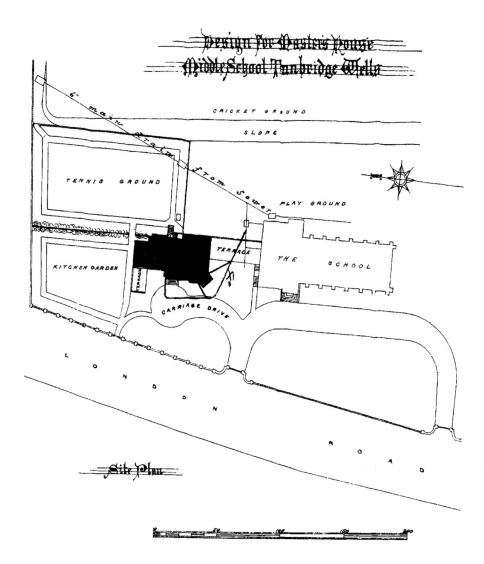

1889 Plan showing a Kitchen Garden adjoining the Headmaster's House (now School House), with the original Tennis ground where the New-Wing now is and the Cricket ground beyond.

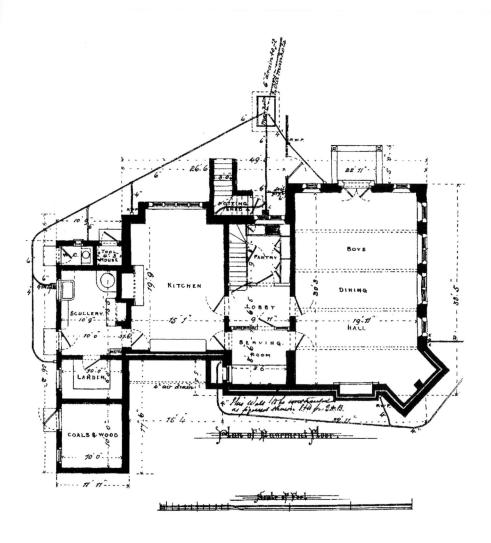

Plan showing the original Boys' Dining Hall
in the basement of the Headmaster's House
(now School House).

NOTES AND REFERENCES for Part II

(1)   Letter of 17.6.1891 from Burnell to the Skinners'
        Company held among the Guildhall manuscripts.

(2)   Obituaries to Burnell appear in the RIBA Journal of
        Proceedings, Vol. 8, No.12, 7.4.1892
        and in The Builder, Vol. 62, 16.4.1892.

(3)   Court of Governors Minute Book, Vol. 1, 2.7.1885.

(4)   Court Minutes, 18.11.1886.

(5)   Court Minutes, 1.8.1889.

(6)   The Tunbridge Wells Journal, 28.10.1886.

(7)   Court Minutes, 18.2.1897.

(8)   Court Minutes, 20.4.1899.

(9)   Court Minutes, 22.6.1899.

(10)   Obituary in RIBA Journal, Vol. 59, 1952.

(11)   Court Minutes, 2.2.1899, 4.5.1899
        and Boys Middle School Committee Minutes, 14.11.1899.

(12)   Bygone Kent, p.694.

(13)   Courier, 16.7.1920.

(14)   Courier, 7.7.1922.

SHORT BIBLIOGRAPHY

Brown, Susan : *Researching Royal Tunbridge Wells* Royal Tunbridge Wells Civic Society Monograph No.2, 2003.

Chapman, Frank : *David Peacock's Tunbridge Wells Sketchbook – 25Years On,* 2003

Ditchfield, F.H. : *The City Companies of London and their good works,* 1904.

Herbert, William : *The History of the Twelve Great Livery Companies of London,* Vol.2, 1836, *reprinted* 1968.

Lambert, John James : *Records of The Skinners of London Edward I to James I,* 1933.

McAuliffe, Everett : Unpublished notes towards a history of The Skinners' School

Pontifex, Bryan : *The City of London Livery Companies,* 1939

Rivington, Septimus : *The History of Tonbridge School,* 1898

Savidge, Alan : *Royal Tunbridge Wells,* 1975.

Thomson, J. Radford : *Pelton's Illustrated Guide to Tunbridge Wells,* 1888

Veale, Elspeth M. : *The English Fur Trade in the Later Middle Ages,* 1966.

INDEX